Waterford port and harbour, 1815–42

Maynooth Studies in Local History

SERIES EDITOR Raymond Gillespie

This volume is one of five short books published in the Maynooth Studies in Local History series in 2019. Like their predecessors they range widely over the local experience in the Irish past. Chronologically they focus on the late eighteenth and nineteenth centuries but they focus on problems that reappeared in almost every period of Irish history. They span the experience of rebellion in late eighteenth-century Dublin and the trauma of family relations and murder in the early nineteenth century. More mundane tasks such as the problem of managing the poor, the task of economic development through the shaping of infrastructure and the management of land also feature. Geographically they range across the length of the country from Dublin to Waterford by way of Carlow and westwards from Howth to Sligo. Socially they move from those living on the margins of society in Sligo through the urban middle classes of mid nineteenth-century Dublin to the prosperous world of the urban elite in Waterford. In doing so they reveal diverse and complicated societies that created the local past and present the range of possibilities open to anyone interested in studying that past. Those possibilities involve the dissection of the local experience in the complex and contested social worlds of which it is part as people strove to preserve and enhance their positions within their local societies. It also reveals the forces that made for cohesion in local communities and those that drove people apart, whether through large scale rebellion or through acts of inter-personal violence. Such studies of local worlds over such long periods are vital for the future since they not only stretch the historical imagination but provide a longer perspective on the development of society in Ireland and help us to understand more fully the complex evolution of the Irish experience. These works do not simply chronicle events relating to an area within administrative or geographically determined boundaries, but open the possibility of understanding how and why particular regions had their own personality in the past. Such an exercise is clearly one of the most exciting challenges for the future and demonstrates the vitality of the study of local history in Ireland.

Maynooth Studies in Local History: Number 140

Waterford port and harbour, 1815–42

Mary Breen

FOUR COURTS PRESS

Set in 10pt on 12pt Bembo by
Carrigboy Typesetting Services for
FOUR COURTS PRESS LTD
7 Malpas Street, Dublin 8, Ireland
www.fourcourtspress.ie
and in North America for
FOUR COURTS PRESS
c/o IPG, 814 N Franklin St, Chicago, IL 60610

© Mary Breen and Four Courts Press 2019

ISBN 978–1–84682–800–3

All rights reserved. Without limiting the rights under
copyright reserved alone, no part of this publication may
be reproduced, stored in or introduced into a retrieval system,
or transmitted, in any form or by any means (electronic,
mechanical, photocopying, recording or otherwise), without
the prior written permission of both the copyright
owner and the above publisher of this book.

Printed in Ireland
by SprintPrint, Dublin.

Contents

Acknowledgments

This short book is based on research for the degree of MA in Irish History at NUI Maynooth. I owe a debt of gratitude to my thesis supervisor Professor Raymond Gillespie for his encouragement, guidance and advice. As series editor of Maynooth Studies in Local History, Professor Gillespie has been instrumental in bringing this book to fruition and I wish to express my sincere thanks. I am grateful for the constant support received from the members of the history department NUI Maynooth, particularly Professor Marian Lyons and Dr Jacinta Prunty. My research was facilitated by the staff in the various repositories and libraries I visited. I would like to thank Brian Donnelly, senior archivist, National Archives of Ireland, for facilitating access to the records of Waterford Harbour Commissioners and for his help in locating relevant sources, and Joanne Rothwell, Archivist, Waterford City and County Council, for access to the records of Waterford Corporation and Waterford Chamber of Commerce. I also acknowledge the assistance of Eamonn McEneaney and the staff of Waterford Museum of Treasures, the staff of the National Library of Ireland, Trinity College Library, and Waterford City Library. I am grateful to Brian Moore, Port of Waterford Company, for access to the seal of Waterford Harbour Commissioners, and to Eddie O'Keeffe for his sketch of the building that housed Waterford Harbour Commissioners. On a personal level I wish to thank my family and friends, who have been a constant source of encouragement and support over the years. This book is dedicated to my late father Jimmy Daly, who worked in the port of Waterford, and my late husband Ernie Breen, who nurtured my interest in Waterford history.

Introduction

This study explores the management and operation of the port and harbour of Waterford in the period 1815 to 1842. In 1815, the ongoing tensions and strife between the body representing the merchants and traders of Waterford and the municipal corporation regarding the management and operation of the port and harbour escalated. The dispute culminated in the introduction of an act of parliament in 1816 removing the responsibility for the management of the port from the unreformed corporation of Waterford, and placing the stewardship of the port and harbour with a new statutory body, Waterford Harbour Commissioners. The establishment, composition, responsibilities and performance of this new body is at the heart of this book, but the research also addresses Waterford Corporation and Waterford Chamber of Commerce, both chartered bodies, and their relationship and interactions. The story begins in 1815 on the eve of the establishment of Waterford Harbour Commissioners and ends in early 1842, at which point Waterford Corporation, and all other Irish municipal corporations, began to experience the impact of the reforms instigated by the Municipal Corporations (Ireland) Act of 1840.[1] Furthermore, within a short period the act that established Waterford Harbour Commissioners became the subject of a review and was replaced by an act of 1846 that reconstituted the harbour board and gave the commissioners additional powers.[2]

The trade and commerce of the city of Waterford was focused on its river, port and harbour. Waterford city is situated on the river Suir, and the river and its harbour have been central to the city's history and development. The 'gentle' Suir rises on the eastern flanks of Benduff Mountain in the Devil's Bit range, Co. Tipperary, and flows for 115 miles, passing through the towns of Thurles, Cahir, Clonmel, and Carrick-on-Suir, until finally it 'adorns rich Waterford',[3] where it enters the sea at Waterford Harbour in the company of the rivers Nore and Barrow. The Suir is tidal to beyond Carrick-on-Suir, navigable to Clonmel, and grants access to considerable fertile inland areas. Vessels exiting Waterford Harbour, on Ireland's south-east coast, have easy access to some of the most heavily traversed maritime routes in British and Irish waters.

This study identifies the forces at play in the management and operation of the port and harbour of Waterford in the period from 1815 to 1842, and assesses their stewardship of the infrastructure and facilities central to the economic and mercantile development of the city and its hinterland. It also explores the tensions between the political and mercantile elites and the bodies that represented them, as they struggled to retain their exclusivity and influence in a period where political and social reforms resulted in shifting power relations between the numerically inferior, but politically dominant, Protestants, and Catholics who began to make substantial gains in power and influence. It is fortunate that the minute books for the three bodies at the heart of this study are extant for the period under consideration. The minute books of Waterford Harbour Commissioners (uninterrupted for this period) are held in the National Archives of Ireland, while the complete minute books of Waterford Corporation and the (almost complete) minute books of Waterford Chamber of Commerce are held by Waterford City and County Archives. They provide a record of the relevant decisions of these bodies in relation to the port, harbour and commerce of the city. They also provide some insights into the relationships between the three bodies. The National Archives holds a wealth of material relating to Waterford Harbour Commissioners, including letter books, charts, pilotage books, daily reports of weather conditions maintained by the pilot master, accounts, correspondence and legal documentation. However, the material is largely uncatalogued and stored in boxes in loosely tied bundles, making it somewhat difficult to locate relevant material. Nevertheless, these records are a rich source of material for this book.

Parliamentary papers have been used to trace the extent and growth of trade at Waterford and other Irish ports. In particular reports of tonnage and shipping, and the reports of the commissioners for auditing public accounts in Ireland have been used. The latter, together with the annual accounts published in local newspapers, were useful for gaining an insight into the income and expenditure of Waterford Harbour Commissioners and the works undertaken by them. The journals of the house of commons, the reports of the Directors General of Inland Navigation in Ireland, the tidal harbour commissioners report of 1846, the 1835 report of the commissioners appointed to inquire into municipal corporations, and the report of the 1930 ports and harbours tribunal, have provided important background information and comparison data. The 1835 report was also invaluable in providing a record of the abuses of privilege perpetrated by the municipal corporations, including Waterford Corporation.

As the records of Waterford Harbour Commissioners, Waterford Corporation and Waterford Chamber of Commerce are very formal documents, largely recording resolutions, they lack the detail necessary to provide a comprehensive picture of the attitudes of the politicians and merchants to each other and their concerns, but contemporary local newspapers provide additional context. Two newspapers in particular have been useful. The *Waterford Chronicle* began publication *c.*1756 and continued from *c.*1790 to 1823 as *Ramsey's Waterford Chronicle*, and then became, until 1844, the *Waterford Chronicle*. Its content was influenced by its ownership. Until 1823 it was owned by a liberal Protestant but from 1824 it was owned by the Barrons, a Catholic family and supporters of Daniel O'Connell and the fight for Catholic Emancipation. The *Waterford Mail* commenced publication in 1823. It was owned by Robert Fleury and reflected the conservative Protestant viewpoint.[4]

A number of histories of Irish ports and their respective Harbour Commissioners have been written. While these have been of interest for comparison purposes, most are general works covering periods of up to 200 years. Ned McHugh's detailed account of Drogheda port in the period from 1790 to 1850 has been of particular interest and proved very useful in highlighting possible source material for this book.[5] Cormac Ó Gráda, Joel Mokyr and L.M. Cullen have written extensively about the Irish economy of the period.[6] Their writings offer a broader picture of the Irish economy and trade, and provide context for this study of Waterford port and harbour.

Several detailed studies of various aspects of Waterford history and society in the first half of the 19th century have been published. Eugene Broderick's research on Waterford's Anglicans between 1819 and 1872 exposed the concerns and pressures facing the Anglican community in this period,[7] and many of the individuals who grace his pages were members of one, and in some cases all, of the bodies central to this study. Broderick's study of the unreformed corporation of Waterford has afforded a valuable insight into the mind-set of that body.[8] Elizabeth A. Heggs' PhD thesis, which focused on the distinctive nature of Waterford Protestantism in the period, has also been of value.[9] J.M. Hearne's study of Waterford's economy, society and politics during the period has been indispensable for providing an examination of the performance of the Waterford economy in relation to the Irish economy in general and for its exploration of patterns of engagement in Waterford trade.[10] A number of articles published in *Waterford, History and Society* have aided the writing of this study, particularly Peter Solar's study of the agricultural trade of Waterford port between 1809 and 1909.[11] Solar's analysis of Irish shipping and economic development in the 19th century provided a much-needed lesson in the vagaries of shipping statistics.[12] Eamonn McEneaney's general history of Waterford's mayors proved beneficial.[13] Bill Irish's *Shipbuilding in Waterford, 1820–1882*, contains a plethora of detail on the economic and political background of the period and an insight into industry and society in Waterford in the first half of the 19th century, particularly the role of Quaker entrepreneurs in Waterford industry.[14]

While much has been written and published about aspects of the unreformed corporation of Waterford in the early 19th century, the same attention has not been paid to the other two bodies, the subject of this small book. In 1988, Des Cowman provided a brief general history of 200 years of the activities of Waterford Chamber of Commerce, highlighting the tensions between the chamber and the corporation.[15] Anthony Brophy has published extracts from the records of Waterford Harbour Commissioners in *Decies* and these extracts piqued the interest of the present writer.[16]

The first chapter of the present work considers the Irish and Waterford economy on the eve of the 19th century and sets out the national and local challenges facing the economy and trade. It also explores the relationship between the parties with a stake in the management and development of the port

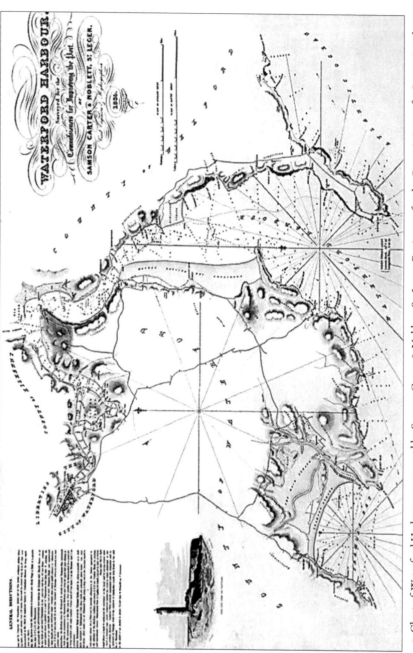

1. Chart of Waterford Harbour, as surveyed by Samson Carter & Nobbett St. Leger, Engineers, for the Commissioners for Improving the Port of Waterford, 1835. Source: www.whytes.ieart1835-chart-of-waterford

and harbour of Waterford in the early 19th century, and assesses the political and mercantile factors, both local and national, that influenced the establishment in 1816 of a new statutory body, Waterford Harbour Commissioners, to manage the port and harbour of Waterford. The second chapter considers the reactions of Waterford Corporation, a stronghold of Protestant power and favour that jealously and reflexively guarded its rights and privileges from encroachment by other bodies, and Waterford Chamber of Commerce, a body that resented the corporation's chartered rights and privileges and their neglect of the port and harbour, to the bill before parliament proposing to grant power over the port and harbour to a third body. This chapter is also concerned with the composition and interests of the newly appointed Waterford Harbour Commissioners and the powers and responsibilities placed on them by the act of 1816. The third chapter analyses the manner in which Waterford Harbour Commissioners fulfilled their responsibilities under the enabling act of 1816 during the 26–year period to 1842. The purpose of the act of parliament of 1816 was to improve the port and harbour of Waterford as this would 'tend to promote the trade and commerce of the said city',[17] and consequently the chapter will assess the fortunes of Waterford's economy and trade over the period of the study. As the act of 1816 was primarily concerned with improvements and access to the port of Waterford, this study focuses on this area including the quays at Waterford and extending as far as King's or Little Island, some two miles downstream of the city.

1. The mercantile, political and economic arena: Waterford port and harbour in the early 19th century

With certain exceptions, the Irish economy of the early 19th century was predominantly agricultural. In addition to feeding its own growing population, a large part of the country's agricultural produce was exported, mainly to British markets.[1] Tillage farming provided the raw material for Ireland's milling, distilling and brewing industries, and changes introduced in agricultural methods in the late 18th century facilitated the growth of these industries, which were predominantly southern-based.[2] As Ireland's road network was seriously deficient and its rail network was in its infancy, the movement of produce and raw materials within the island relied on coastal shipping, the canals and the rivers. Ireland was not generously bestowed with raw materials and natural resources, and accordingly the ports were important for industries that depended on imported materials.[3] These industries, such as the glass industry, tended to be based in the port towns and cities, as did mills and distilleries, many of which were established in towns along the rivers discharging into the main ports. Ireland had an export-oriented economy, and all of its trade with other countries relied on transportation by ship, making its ports and harbours crucial to the economic future of the country.

For most of the 18th century, Waterford was the third-busiest port in Ireland, after Dublin and Cork.[4] The city, situated on the river Suir, near the confluence of that river with the rivers Nore and Barrow, 'was the natural outlet for the produce of the rich valleys' of the three sister rivers.[5] The city was also conveniently close to some of the busiest maritime routes in British and Irish waters.[6] As a result of ties created by migration, inter-marriage, familial, business and commercial interactions and interests, Waterford merchants were part of an elaborate international mercantile network. Waterford ships traded with England, mainland Europe, and the West Indies.[7] The city was the main centre of the Newfoundland provisions trade, which accounted for between 10 and 15 per cent of Waterford's exports.[8] Over the 18th century, Waterford's butter exports increased from 8,851 to 79,455 hundredweight per annum, beef exports increased from 3,157 to 13,735 barrels per annum, and pork exports, insignificant in 1700, rose to 13,138 barrels in the year 1790.[9] Most of the legislation enacted to penalize Ireland economically had either been repealed or had ceased to be enforced by the last quarter of the 18th century, and the Irish economy entered a period of rapid growth.

Waterford benefited from this expansion of the economy,[10] and the resultant affluence is reflected in the architecture of Georgian Waterford. The Anglican cathedral, the townhouse of the Morris family, City Hall, the Bishop's Palace, and the Catholic cathedral (an ambitious undertaking wherein Waterford's Catholics petitioned the exclusively Protestant corporation for land on which to build Ireland's first post-Reformation Catholic cathedral) were all constructed in this period.[11] In 1793, the first bridge, a wooden structure, was built over the Suir, upstream of the city quays.[12] One contemporary writer considered that the quay in Waterford, at which ships loaded and unloaded, 'is not inferior to, but rather exceeds the most celebrated in Europe'.[13]

A fundamental factor for the survival of Waterford port was its ability to compete with other Irish ports. With the increasing orientation of trade towards the British market, proximity to the great ports of Britain was a critical factor for individual Irish ports, as were the extent and richness of the hinterland the port could access; the navigable quality of the river on which the port was built; the capacity, efficiency and viability of the port and harbour infrastructure; and the quality of port management. In the case of Waterford, the nearby ports of New Ross and Youghal did not threaten the viability of the port; Waterford's main competitors were Cork and Limerick for the trade of Co. Limerick and western Co. Tipperary, and Dublin for the trade of Cos Carlow and Laois.[14] While Waterford was closer to Britain than Cork, Waterford suffered from its proximity to Dublin, a factor that did not affect Cork.[15] By 1790, almost 50 per cent of Ireland's butter exports passed through Cork,[16] at which time Waterford exported the second-highest value of such exports – accounting for 26.4 per cent of all exported Irish butter (the Waterford exports were valued at £250,000 per annum).[17] Waterford's nearest competitor, the port of Cork, made great strides in the closing years of the 18th century, aided by the fact that it was sheltered from competition with Dublin; Cork's rich agricultural hinterland provided a ready supply of butter for its highly organized butter market, and its worldwide export trade grew significantly.[18] Between the years 1776 and 1800, an average of 96,680 tons of shipping per annum passed through the port of Cork, compared with 38,302 tons per annum at Waterford port.[19] By the final year of the 18th century, Waterford had slipped from third to fourth place in the ranking of Ireland's ports (table 1), a situation caused by the surge of growth experienced in Belfast, where exports had grown to 50,000 tons per annum.[20]

Table 1. Irish shipping by port: all tonnage entering in the year 1799[21]

Percentage tonnage	Port	Percentage tonnage	Port
41.6	Dublin	6.9	Newry
20.0	Cork	3.7	Drogheda
10.3	Belfast	3.0	Londonderry
7.1	**Waterford**	7.4	Combined tonnage entering other ports

As a major commercial centre, a key factor in the success of Waterford's trade and commercial life was the operation of its port and harbour, the responsibility for which rested with Waterford Municipal Corporation. The Act of Union of 1800 had reduced the number of such corporations from 117 to 69.[22] These bodies operated under charters granted by the crown. The governing charter for all aspects of civic life in Waterford, until the introduction of the Municipal Corporation (Ireland) Act in 1840, was the charter granted by King Charles I, on 26 May 1626.[23] This charter granted to the mayor, sheriffs, and citizens of Waterford (the municipal corporation) and their successors forever:

> the great port of the city of Waterford ... between the ingress and entrance thereof between Rodybanke and Rindoane, and from thence to Carrigmagriffin; and all the water betwixt the said bounds, and the land and soil covered with water, or being between the flowing and ebbing of the sea within the said bounds.[24]

In Waterford, the merchant community consisted primarily of members of the landed gentry and the middle classes.[25] There existed an active committee of merchants who began meeting in 1787,[26] and in 1805 formed themselves into the Waterford Chamber of Commerce.[27] Membership of the chamber of commerce was restricted to persons who were either 'merchants, traders or bankers'.[28] The majority of the merchants were members of the established church, but there were a significant number of Catholic and Quaker merchants, ensuring that 'Waterford's economic elite were more socially and religiously diverse than Waterford Corporation'.[29]

Chambers of Commerce came into being to represent the merchant community, driven by local demands to articulate the concerns of the merchants and by the 'perceived inattentiveness of government'.[30] It has been argued that the catalyst for the development of the first chambers of commerce in Ireland and Britain was the need to voice the disapproval and concern of the merchant community at government policies and actions that disrupted international trade.[31] The first chambers in Ireland, and a large percentage of Britain's chambers (70 to 80 per cent), were established in major port towns and cities. In the late 18th and early 19th centuries a major grievance of most Irish, and indeed British, chambers was the manner in which local municipal corporations set and collected harbour dues, and maintained harbours, roads, wharfs, quays, and other infrastructure necessary to ensure that local ports and harbours functioned properly. Liverpool Chamber of Commerce had been established to resist the corporation's dock fees, and opposition and resistance to the abuses and policies of their respective local corporations was the spark for the creation of the Londonderry, and Cork, chambers of commerce.[32] The chambers gave voice to mercantile concerns by lobbying politicians and government, by representing the interests of their members, by informing their members on relevant issues of the day, and by corresponding with, and on occasion supporting the petitions of, other chambers. Many merchants were excluded from politics in this period by virtue of their religion, and membership of the chamber of commerce afforded them a means of organizing and articulating their grievances against both local and national government.

Early 19th-century municipal corporations have been described as bearing 'a closer resemblance to exclusive clubs ... than to governing bodies'.[33] In the early years of the century, Waterford Chamber of Commerce became increasingly critical of the corporation's stewardship of the port and its infrastructure. Under the governing charter, appointment of many Waterford port officials fell within the gift of the corporation, and a key concern of the merchant community was what they regarded as the inefficient and corrupt nature of appointees, together with the archaic nature of some posts, all of which they considered held no place in the operation and development of a modern, competitive port.[34] While the Waterford butter trade was dominated by Quaker and Catholic merchants, the efficiency with which butter for export was cleared through the port, and the grading of butter quality, was controlled by the Protestant corporation, as this body appointed the weighmaster and butter taster, both of whom received a commission based on the number of firkins weighed and tasted.[35] These were lucrative and influential posts. The charges for weighing butter was 4½*d*. per firkin, 2*d*. of which went to the weighmaster, 1*d*. to the butter taster and the remaining 1½*d*. to the corporation as a custom on butter.[36] The 1835 report into Irish municipal corporations recorded that the butter taster appointed by Waterford Corporation – Sir Nicholas Britiffe Skottowe, one of the original members of Waterford Harbour Commissioners – had not been resident in Waterford for some time, and his duties were carried out by a deputy.[37] In the years from May 1821 to May 1833, the butter taster received an average of £135 per annum, while his deputy received an average of £170 per annum.[38] Irked by these inefficiencies and perceived abuses, the chamber challenged the municipal corporation on several issues including its failure to maintain the city quays and the principal streets of the city; the increased fees charged by the corporation-appointed water bailiff, and illegal tolls levied and collected by the corporation appointee, Sheriff Hassard.[39]

Waterford Chamber of Commerce applied for a royal charter in 1807. The granting of a royal charter was not guaranteed: the Jersey chamber was refused a charter in 1787, and the Dublin chamber contemplated an application in 1823 but decided not to pursue it further.[40] A royal charter conferred status on a chamber and gave them legal parity with the chartered bodies they often lobbied against, the municipal corporations. The Waterford chamber required the charter in order to create a legal entity to operate the debenture structure of shareholders it developed to purchase, in 1812, the building that would become its headquarters, the former Morris townhouse at George's Street, Waterford.[41] Waterford Chamber of Commerce was successful in its application and was granted a royal charter in 1815.[42]

In 1806, the chamber established a committee to report on the state of navigation of the river Suir,[43] and another committee to examine the state of dereliction of the public quays.[44] The committee set up to investigate the Suir consisted of Simon Newport (of the Newport banking family), John Blake and Richard Pope.[45] In December 1806, the report prepared by this committee was submitted to the Directors General of Inland Navigation in Ireland,[46] by Sir John Newport (1756–1843), member of parliament for Waterford (1803–32) and Chancellor of the Irish Exchequer (1806–7).[47]

In addition to serving as member of parliament for Waterford for almost 30 years, John Newport was also a member of Waterford Municipal Corporation and Waterford Chamber of Commerce, the body promoting improvements to Waterford port and harbour. Sir John's father had established a bank in Waterford city in or around 1772.[48] He took his sons into the business, and the bank became known as the bank of 'Simon Newport, Sir John Newport, Bart, and William Newport'.[49] Newport's Bank was the principal bank in the city in the early 19th century.

Sir John left the banking business and moved into politics in the opening years of the 19th century. Along with his father, uncles and brothers, he held positions on Waterford Corporation, and Sir John and his close family were integral to the political and commercial life of Waterford, making him a key figure in the development of the city and in the political landscape of the period. He was chairman of the company, incorporated by an act of parliament, that oversaw the building of the first bridge, 'Timbertoes', over the Suir at Waterford city.[50] Sir John was a liberal Protestant, and he was consistently supportive of the Catholic cause, factors that benefited him politically, particularly when contesting the 1807 election.[51] In his role as MP for Waterford he maintained a lively correspondence with the chamber on issues impacting local mercantile interests such as butter exports, the mail packet service between Waterford and Milford Haven, repeal of the duties on salt and works on the harbour at Dunmore East.[52] While Sir John was assiduous in the attention he paid to all matters of importance to Waterford and Ireland in the London parliament, the means by which he retained his seat in parliament, and also his control over Waterford Corporation between 1818 and his retirement in 1832, can only be described as unscrupulous and self-serving. Between 1818 and 1830, the unreformed corporation of Waterford was controlled by a secret compact between the Newport family and their opponents, the Alcocks.[53] The compact of 1818 between Sir John Newport (then 62 years old) and Harry Alcock, guaranteed Sir John the representation of the city in parliament for life, or for as long as he felt able to serve, after which Newport's support would transfer to Alcock. Consequently, Sir John Newport was re-elected without challenge in 1818, 1820, 1826, 1830 and 1831.[54] Under the agreement, the Newport and Alcock families shared effective control over Waterford Corporation, including the filling of vacancies among the aldermen, appointments to various offices, and 'all acts relating to the making of freemen'.[55]

The report on the state of the river Suir, presented by Sir John Newport to the Directors General of Inland Navigation in 1806, stated that following a survey of the river at King's Channel, a sum of £500 was required immediately to provide rings, buoys, chains and anchors for the safety of ships passing through the channel, and that a further sum of £1,000 was required to carry out works to deepen the channel.[56] The merchants also sought the establishment of a ballast office in the city for the better management of navigation. Sir John Newport promoted the application, and in a letter accompanying the report, pledged that any monies approved for the project would be 'faithfully and honestly expended'.[57] The Board of Inland Navigation confirmed that while the water in the river at King's Channel was very deep, its winding course made passage difficult, and at times impossible.[58] This part of the river is approximately two miles downstream of Waterford city and two miles upstream of the junction of the rivers Suir and Barrow. The course of the Suir is divided in this area by an island known as King's or Little Island. The King's Channel lies to the south of the island, while to the north lies a direct passage, known as 'the Ford'. However, this passage was shallower than the south channel and obstructed by rocks. A sum of £1,500 had been spent in the past on partially clearing the passage, but the 'shoal' had accumulated again.[59]

The Act of Union of 1800 was politically and financially significant for Ireland, but did not have an immediate economic impact.[60] The Irish economy continued to grow, fanned by the demands created by the Napoleonic Wars.[61] However, Waterford's trade suffered as the conflict impeded access to its long-established markets, a demand that was quickly filled by European competitors.[62] In addition, legislation in 1812 enabled the exportation of cheap provisions directly from mainland Europe to the North American colonies, thereby impacting on Waterford merchants engaged in the provisions trade.[63] With the fall in demand for salted meat products, the export of commodities produced from the by-products of slaughtering such as candles, shoes and soap, all lucrative markets, fell dramatically.[64] Irish butter exports continued to grow, with the ports of Waterford and Cork handling most of the country's trade in butter (table 2).

Table 2. Irish butter exports year ended 1 June 1815[65]

Port	Firkins of butter exported	Port	Firkins of butter exported
Cork	300,000	Limerick	30,000
Waterford	**200,000**	Sligo	30,000
Belfast	70,000	Derry/Coleraine	20,000
Newry	70,000	Dundalk	10,000
Dublin	60,000	Drogheda	10,000
Wexford	30,000	New Ross	30,000
		TOTAL	**860,000**

If Waterford was to increase its share of this market, it needed to increase its catchment area, an ambition possible only if the navigation of the Suir and her sister rivers was maintained and improved.[66] A further possible threat to the port of Waterford emerged in evidence given by William Colvill, Esq., of the Barrow Navigation Company to the Directors General of Inland Navigation in 1811, wherein he anticipated that if the Barrow navigation works were completed, and tolls on the Grand Canal reduced as legislation permitted, there would be a 'great increase of trade in corn' along this route and through the port of Dublin to Liverpool, in preference to the corn being exported through Waterford, as the Waterford route would prove 'much more expensive and uncertain'.[67]

On a national level, a number of significant factors impacted on the Irish economy in 1816: Ireland was recovering from the economic crisis and famine conditions of 1810 and the subsequent drop in agricultural prices; the country was facing a drop in the demand for Irish exports with the end of the Napoleonic wars; discussions were ongoing in parliament on the state of Irish debt and the amalgamation of the British and Irish exchequers was under consideration.

These uncertainties, together with the physical condition of the Suir at Waterford, are likely to have influenced the members of Waterford Chamber of Commerce to take measures to improve the competitiveness of the port and harbour. Accordingly, emboldened by the royal charter granted in 1815, the chamber submitted a petition to parliament on 16 February 1816, promoting port improvements. The chief secretary for Ireland, Robert Peel, announced to the house of commons that the Prince Regent, being acquainted with the contents of the petition, commended it to the house for consideration.[68] The purpose of the petition was to seek parliament's assistance in achieving improvements that the petitioners considered vital for the 'great public objects' of the port of Waterford, which afforded 'commercial intercourse to a very large portion of the most fertile districts in Ireland'.[69]

The improvements consisted of the removal of natural impediments in the direct river channel to the city, at a place called the 'Ford', as these impediments were forcing ships, other than those with a very limited draft of water, to navigate a more circuitous channel of the river which contained sunken rocks and dangerous currents. The proposed works consisted of the creation of a new direct channel through the ford, thereby allowing ships of any burden, not exceeding fourteen feet in draft, to navigate a direct approach. The petitioners reminded parliament that they represented a considerable portion of the merchants of Waterford city and that they had recently been 'incorporated by royal letters patent'.[70] They stated that they had dedicated what financial resources they could muster to the advancement of the mercantile interests of the port, but these works, estimated to cost £25,000, while of 'infinite utility', were beyond their means, and the petition proposed that a portion of the estimated cost of the improvement works would be provided from duties levied on local commerce as the immediate beneficiaries of the works, and the balance from a grant of public money by parliament.[71]

The arguments put forward by the merchants of Waterford in favour of their application for public funding for the improvement works were cleverly constructed to demonstrate that the works would benefit the economy and security of the United Kingdom of Great Britain and Ireland. The merchants stated that the annual value of exports passing through the port of Waterford had on several occasions exceeded £2 million sterling in value, and that these exports were primarily destined for Great Britain.[72] This was consistent with the orientation of Irish trade towards British markets from the late 18th century. By 1800, 85 per cent of Irish exports were destined for Britain.[73] Conscious that the authorities were determined to tackle smuggling and maximize the income from duties on imported and exported goods, the petition stressed that the most efficient method of collecting customs and duties from ships and preventing illicit trade was to ensure that ships could berth at the quays of the city.[74] The events of 1798 had shown what a security risk Ireland could be, and the subsequent Act of Union sought to contain this risk. With these factors in mind, the petitioners assured parliament that the depth of water at the quays in Waterford would, if required, permit cavalry to disembark speedily and securely.

However, the merchants and traders of the chamber of commerce did not restrict their petition to a request for public funds 'to effectuate an object in which so considerable a portion of the Kingdom, as well as the due collection of its Revenues, is materially interested'.[75] Their frustration and annoyance at the failure of the corporation to carry out its responsibilities to maintain and manage the port and its infrastructure is likely to have been the catalyst that caused them to request that, for the purpose of funding the necessary improvement works, 'as well as for attaining other considerable improvements respecting ballasting of ships, and the due regulation of pilotage, leave may be given to bring in a Bill explaining all these commercial objects'.[76] Sir John Newport, member of parliament for Waterford, and the members of Waterford Chamber of Commerce were no doubt aware that such a bill in respect of Dublin port, introduced in the Irish parliament on 1 February 1786 by John Beresford, son of Marcus Beresford, later Lord Tyrone, had resulted in an act creating a new board entitled 'The corporation for preserving and improving the Port of Dublin'.[77] Likewise, Drogheda Harbour Commissioners had been created by an act of parliament of 1790. More significantly, the Commercial Building Company of the city of Cork, Waterford's main competitor port, had petitioned parliament in 1813, seeking a bill allowing the levying of 'one British shilling' on all vessels entering and leaving the port of Cork in order to fund commercial improvements within the city and port of Cork.[78] The petition resulted in an act of parliament of 1814 that appointed the mayor, sheriffs and certain individuals as commissioners for widening, deepening and improving the harbour and river of Cork.[79] Therefore, the creation of a separate body for the management of Waterford port and harbour, which would dilute the influence of the municipal corporation over the port and harbour, is likely to have been the aim of the promoters of the Waterford petition.

Parliament ordered that the petition be considered by a committee headed by Sir John Newport and Sir Robert Peel.[80] The committee reported on 14 March 1816 and the following day parliament granted leave to bring in a bill for improvements to the port and harbour of Waterford and related matters.[81] The members of Waterford Chamber of Commerce must have been heartened by the fact that preparation of this bill was delegated to the MP for Waterford city, Sir John Newport, and the MP for the borough of Dungarvan, Co. Waterford, General George Walpole.[82] Walpole was a Whig supporter, and like Sir John Newport, he consistently voted in favour of relief measures for Catholics.[83] While the bill was being prepared by Newport and Walpole, parliament resolved on 20 March 1816 that the Irish treasury should advance a loan out of the consolidated fund for Ireland to the Directors General for Inland Navigation and to certain commissioners to be appointed by an act of parliament.[84] Newport and Walpole were instructed to make provision for these matters in the bill. Sir John Newport presented a draft bill for improving the port and harbour of Waterford for a first reading on 25 March 1816, proposing the creation of a separate board of commissioners to manage Waterford port and harbour, which would effectively remove the control and influence of Waterford Corporation over the management and operation of the port and harbour.

While the trade and commerce of Waterford flourished in the 18th century, by the 1810s Waterford's economic future was facing both internal and external threats. Due to the export-oriented nature of the Irish and Waterford economies, a properly functioning and managed port and harbour was crucial. The early 19th century saw the commencement of a series of actions by the merchants of Waterford Chamber of Commerce with a view to improving the operation, management and infrastructure of Waterford port and harbour in order to secure the competitiveness and future of the port. Their actions brought them into conflict with the municipal corporation of Waterford, a body that jealously guarded its powers and functions, while at the same time often neglecting to implement such powers and functions, thereby giving credence to the conclusion of the royal commission of inquiry set up in 1833 to inquire into Irish municipal corporations: that such bodies were 'in many instances of no service to the community; in all, insufficient and inadequate to the proper purposes and ends of such institutions'.[85] The events detailed above highlight the pervasive influence of the elected MP for Waterford, Sir John Newport; the growing power and influence of the merchant representative body, the chamber of commerce; and the close connections between chambers and the manner in which they influenced each other. In 1816, the reform agenda of the Whig government was not sufficiently developed to implement widespread reform and meaningful funding of municipal government. Consequently, the petitioning of parliament by the chamber of commerce, supported and aided by

Sir John Newport, resulted in a local act to establish a new body to manage the port and harbour of Waterford. The battle between the two competing forces – Waterford Chamber of Commerce and Waterford Municipal Corporation – for control over the port and harbour of Waterford as this bill wound its way through the legislative process will be explored in the following chapter.

2. The establishment of Waterford Harbour Commissioners in 1816

Before the bill before parliament to improve the port and harbour of Waterford could be read a second time, the corporation reacted swiftly to the proposals that would encroach on their chartered privileges and interfere with their patronage rights. The corporation submitted a petition to parliament seeking leave to present their objections, and parliament agreed on 8 April 1816 to hear the petitioners when the bill was read a second time.[1]

The initial response of the chamber to the corporation's petition was to attempt to resolve the matter in an amicable manner by seeking a 'friendly explanation' as to why the corporation was opposed to a proposal that would be 'so highly beneficial to the community at large and to this city in particular'.[2] This amiability soon gave way to acrimony, as the corporation responded by questioning the motives of the chamber in promoting the bill, and by warning of increased taxes and costs should the bill be passed.[3] The chamber responded by circulating notices to the citizens of Waterford that sought to reassure them that the rumours circulating in the city suggesting that the bill before parliament, if enacted, would 'greatly enhance the price of coals, and other articles of general consumption', were unfounded, and they clarified that the proposed 'low' tonnage duty to be applied to vessels trading in the port was necessary to repay the loan being advanced and 'to keep the Ford for ever clear of obstruction'.[4] They went on to promise that these charges would be reduced by at least one half when the loan was repaid, and estimated that the tonnage duty would cost customers no more than one halfpenny on a barrel of coals while the loan was being repaid, and no more than one farthing per barrel thereafter.[5] They assured the citizens of Waterford that the 'purely commercial' provisions of the proposed act could not be placed in hands more likely to 'discharge them faithfully' than those of the commissioners proposed under the act, commissioners who would not make the provisions of the act 'a medium of undue patronage, or an engine of political influence',[6] thereby attacking the exclusive nature of the corporation and their abuse of power. The members of the chamber expressed the opinion that the corporation and their supporters cared more for ancient privileges than for the advancement of the city, as in opposing the bill they 'may congratulate themselves on having done more to impede the city of Waterford than the labours of another country may achieve'.[7] It certainly appears that in their efforts to buttress their traditional rights and privileges, the municipal corporation lost sight of the commercial benefits that would accrue to the city and its hinterland from the financial investment in the port and harbour to be delivered under the proposed legislation.

The mayor considered that the notices circulated by the chamber were intended 'to prejudice the public against the corporation', and he responded by publishing notices clarifying that the municipal corporation's opposition to the proposed harbour bill was motivated by a desire to preserve the ancient rights and privileges granted to the corporation under charter, and stating that it was unprecedented that the bill contained no provisions to save the 'rights of any persons or bodies corporate or politic'.[8]

Somewhat belatedly, the corporation seemed to realize what was at stake, as the mayor stated that the corporation did not wish to oppose those elements of the bill that would ensure the commercial success of the port, and sought to have the bill amended, rather than defeated.[9] The major concern of the corporation, expressed by the mayor in an open letter to the citizens, was that under the bill 'none but members of the chamber of commerce' were eligible to be elected commissioners, and the corporation objected to the fact that significant powers would be entrusted to the merchant body with little oversight, as the bill did not appear to grant the Directors of Inland Navigation, also proposed as commissioners, the 'slightest control over the members of the chamber of commerce, to whom such extensive powers are entrusted'.[10]

The deputy mayor called a meeting of the citizens of the city in the assembly rooms on 18 April 1816 to facilitate consideration of the bill.[11] An indication of the concern of the public with the various rumours and counter-rumours is evident from the large attendance, but this may also reflect the fact that both the corporation and the chamber were determined that their supporters would be present. Members from both bodies spoke at the meeting.[12] John Harris from the chamber of commerce outlined the efforts of the chamber to obtain sufficient monies from government for the improvement of the Suir and highlighted the role of Sir John Newport in this endeavour.[13] The chamber appear to have decided that the only way to ensure the bill was passed unopposed was to take a conciliatory attitude towards the municipal corporation, and it is clear that behind-the-scene efforts had been made to remove the provisions that were most repugnant to the corporation – provisions that had clearly been placed in the bill by drafters Sir John Newport and General George Walpole with the intention of excluding the corporation and putting control of the port in the hands of the merchants. When addressing the meeting, Harris acknowledged that the original bill contained several objectionable provisions, all of which had now been purged, with the result that the amended bill now before parliament provided that seven commissioners would be selected from among the corporation.[14] This removed one of the main reasons for opposition from the municipal corporation: the absence of municipal corporation representation on the new body created to manage the port. Following a vote, it was agreed that a petition of the citizens would be transmitted to parliament consenting to the bill, as amended.[15]

While these issues were playing out in public, the matter of the water bailiff's office and fees, a major preoccupation of the corporation, appears to have been the subject of behind-the-scenes negotiations. The position of water bailiff was recognized in the charter of 1626, and the first reference to the fees of the water bailiff in corporation records dates to 18 October 1628.[16] The duties of the post included controlling vessels mooring in the port; providing stages and planks to facilitate the loading and unloading of vessels and providing barrels to coal vessels, duties for which the water bailiff collected fees.

While the corporation may have been negligent in the upkeep and improvement of the port and harbour, they continued to appoint a water bailiff or at times two, as allowed by the charter, who in turn collected fees for carrying out the duties of the post.[17] This situation would become unworkable, and perhaps, as discussed below, illegal, after the enactment of legislation that proposed to place the management of the port and harbour under a new body, with the power to levy fees and duties. Therefore, it is possible that the issue of the powers and duties of the water bailiff helped provide the leverage needed by the corporation to insist that they be given representation on the new harbour authority.[18]

The sequence of events is somewhat unclear, but it appears that the corporation and the commissioners named in the bill before parliament entered into an agreement on 15 May 1816 (Appendix 2).[19] The purpose of the agreement appears to have been to ensure that the bill would proceed without further opposition and without legal challenge. The agreement acknowledged that a bill was before parliament for the improvement of Waterford port and harbour, and that it had been agreed between the commissioners named in the bill and the corporation (possibly around the time of the public announcement in April 1816 by John Harris of the removal of the objectionable provisions of the bill), that 'all the powers and fees of the water bailiff should be vested in the commissioners', in return for which the commissioners would pay the municipal corporation the sum of £400 per annum in perpetuity,[20] effectively a scheme to buy out the water bailiff post and compensate the corporation. The agreement of 15 May 1816 stated that it now appeared that this arrangement was in danger of creating difficulties for the bill's passage. The nature of the possible 'difficulties' is not clear but may relate to the legality of the proposed vesting in a new authority of the fees and powers of the water bailiff, a post within the sole gift of the corporation under the charter, and an appointment that was made, not in perpetuity, but 'during the pleasure' of the corporation.[21] It was now agreed on 15 May 1816 that all references to the water bailiff should be expunged from the bill and that a 'saving of the water bailiff's fees rights and powers be introduced into the said bill in lieu thereof'.[22] It was further agreed that when the bill was enacted, the commissioners would lease from the corporation, in perpetuity, the water bailiff's place, and all the powers and duties of the office, subject to the terms and conditions set out in the draft bill.[23] The bill for improving the port and harbour of Waterford was further discussed in parliament at a number of sittings. Amendments were made, one of which included a section to give effect to the above agreement:

> And it be further enacted, that nothing in this act contained shall extend or be construed to extend, to prejudice or derogate from any rights, interests, privileges, franchises, or authority of the King's Majesty, His Heirs or Successors, or any Body Politic or Corporate, or any of the Water Bailiff or Water Bailiffs of the said City of *Waterford*, or any other Person or Persons whatsoever, except as in this Act especially provided and enacted.[24]

On 12 June 1816, parliament approved the bill,[25] and the act for improving the port and harbour of Waterford was passed into law on 20 June 1816.[26] The local and personal act of 1816, instigated and promoted by the merchants and traders of Waterford Chamber of Commerce, under the guiding hand of Sir John Newport, established Waterford Harbour Commissioners, a body with perpetual succession.[27] The preamble to the act specified that its purpose was to further promote the trade of the port and city, which had increased considerably, by cleaning, deepening and improving that part of the river Suir as constituted the port and harbour, between Bilberry Rock and Hook Tower, including St John's Pill, and to create a fund to defray the cost of the necessary works.[28]

Table 3. Harbour authority membership: Belfast, Drogheda, Cork and Waterford

Harbour authority	Membership
Belfast	Arthur, 5th earl of Donegall, John Foster, speaker of the Irish house of commons, and John Beresford, chief commissioner of revenue in the Irish parliament (the above members never attended meetings), and also 12 leading merchants and shipowners.[29]
Drogheda	The mayor and recorder of Drogheda, the representatives in parliament for the time being for the said town, also the representatives in parliament for the time being for the counties of Meath and Louth, and six aldermen, and seven members of the common council of the corporation of said town.[30]
Cork	The mayor and sheriffs of the city of Cork for the time being, and 21 merchants of the city of Cork. Revised in 1820 as follows: Mayor, sheriffs and five members of the common council and 25 merchants of the city of Cork.[31]
Waterford	**The directors of Inland Navigation of Ireland. Seven members of the common council of the municipal corporation of the city of Waterford; 12 members representing the chamber of commerce of the city of Waterford, and five merchants and inhabitants of the town of Clonmel.[32]**

The act provided that the Directors General of Inland Navigation for the time being would be commissioners and appointed a further 24 commissioners representing three separate vested interests: seven members representing the Common Council of the municipal corporation of the city of Waterford, twelve members representing the chamber of commerce of the city of Waterford and five merchants and inhabitants of the town of Clonmel.[33]

The composition of Waterford Harbour Commissioners differed from the harbour authorities that had been created in Belfast in 1785, Drogheda in 1790 and Cork in 1813 as detailed in table 3 above.

Except for Drogheda, the composition of the above authorities reflects the increasing influence of the merchant communities, and a desire to reduce municipal corporation control over the ports. The merchant representation outnumbered the corporation representation significantly on Waterford Harbour Commissioners, suggesting that the intention was to ensure that the merchants would be able to out-vote the corporation members. This is reflected also in the provisions for making bye-laws under the act, as the act stipulated that such bye-laws could only be enacted if they received the approval of two-thirds of the commissioners present at the meeting to which the proposed bye-laws were presented.[34] Again, this section of the act appears to have been drafted to ensure that the merchant representatives had the final say in the wording and approval of such bye-laws, as the adoption or amendment of such regulations required that 13 commissioners be present at the meeting and that two-thirds of those vote in favour.[35] However, the reality was that the merchants representing the town of Clonmel rarely attended meetings. In February 1823, the commissioners issued written notice to 'the commissioners who are resident in Clonmel' informing them that unless they attended the meetings of the board, the practice of forwarding them copies of the proceedings of meetings would cease.[36] For all practical purposes, Waterford Harbour Commissioners consisted of a board of 19 members, made up of 12 merchants and seven members of the municipal corporation.[37] As the years progressed, meetings were often adjourned due to the failure of sufficient members to attend, and this had repercussions in 1830, as will be discussed below.

The act specified how vacancies caused by death, resignation or absence of commissioners were to be filled. Just as the 1785 act creating a new authority to manage the port of Dublin was greatly influenced by George Beresford, who promoted and drafted the bill,[38] the hand of John Newport is evident in the act to improve the port of Waterford. Both men named themselves as commissioners, and the arrangements for filling vacancies by co-option in the bodies established under both acts created a 'closed shop'.[39] The Waterford Harbour Commissioners were empowered to appoint officers, other than the master pilot, deputy master pilots and pilots, and the act included a variety of additional provisions considered necessary in order that the commissioners might achieve the purposes of the act.[40]

In accordance with the resolution of the house of commons on 20 March 1816,[41] the Irish Treasury was empowered to advance a loan, not exceeding £10,000.[42] The loan was to be advanced to the Directors General of Inland Navigation in Ireland and the harbour commissioners, and was to be used to carry out the necessary works to improve the port and harbour. The monies advanced were to be repaid by the harbour commissioners from duties imposed on those using the port, and the act addressed rates and classes of duties. While the necessary works were in the course of planning and construction, sole responsibility for their management and the management of all expenditure and the employment of persons was to rest with the Directors General of Inland Navigation, and the commissioners were debarred from any interference or control.[43] When the works were completed, they were to be vested in the harbour commissioners.[44] These arrangements provide a context for the appointment of the Directors of Inland Navigation as Waterford Harbour Commissioners.

An aspect of the Waterford Harbour Act of 1816 that was to cause contention was that while the act entrusted the management of the port and harbour to Waterford Harbour Commissioners, the ownership of the quays and areas associated with the port and harbour, including the foreshore, was claimed by Waterford Corporation under the governing charter of 1626. Furthermore, the act explicitly undertook not 'to prejudice or derogate from any rights, interests, privileges, franchises, or authority … of any body politic or corporate'.[45] After the enactment of the act of 1816, the corporation moved quickly to assert their rights over the quays by resolving that while it was considered expedient to place the care and maintenance of the quays under the auspices of the harbour commissioners, the commissioners were not empowered to carry out any works without the consent of the corporation.[46] Subsequent Harbour Acts left intact the ownership rights of the municipal authority, which led to ongoing disagreements between the harbour commissioners and the corporation regarding jurisdiction over the quays and foreshore. In 1930, Sir Henry J. Forde, chairman of Waterford Harbour Commissioners, giving evidence to the Ports and Harbours Tribunal, stated that during his long connection with the harbour commissioners:

> there has been strife sometimes of a bitter nature between the Corporation and the Harbour Board due to the claims made by the Corporation on the shipping revenues and the foreshore rights.[47]

The Drogheda Harbour Act of 1797 empowered the harbour commissioners to purchase and improve waste ground adjoining the river, and to lay claim to certain waste lands remaining unclaimed at the expiry of a specified short period.[48] It has been asserted that these powers enabled Drogheda Harbour Commissioners to transform the quayside landscape.[49] The Ports and Harbours

Tribunal Report 1930 concluded that only in Dublin and Waterford did the situation pertain where a statutory harbour authority existed, but the foreshore and bed or soil of the river were vested in the municipal authority under 'ancient royal charters'.[50]

The 1816 act named 24 men, in addition to the Directors General of Inland Navigation, as the first commissioners charged with responsibility for 'carrying into effect the provisions of this act' (table 4).[51] Each commissioner was obliged to take an oath affirming that he would act 'without favour, affection or sinister motive whatsoever'.[52]

Table 4. Commissioners named in the Waterford Harbour Act, 1816[53]

Representing the common council of the corporation of Waterford	Representing the corporation of the chamber of commerce of the city of Waterford	Representing the merchants and inhabitants of Clonmel
Cornelius Bolton	Right Hon. Sir John Newport	Arthur Riall
Harry Alcock	Henry Holdsworth Hunt	David Malcomson
James Wallace	John Harris	James Morton
Michael Evelyn	Jeremiah Ryan	Robert Banfield
Sir Nicholas Britiffe Skottowe	Edward Courtenay	Robert Grubb
Edmund Skottowe	Richard Davis	
Cornelius Henry Bolton	Joseph Strangman	
	John Leonard	
	Robert Jacob	
	John Strangman	
	George Penrose Ridgway	
	Francis Davis	
and the Directors General of Inland Navigation in Ireland for the time being.		

The 24 commissioners explicitly named in the act of 1816 represented Waterford Municipal Corporation (seven commissioners), Waterford Chamber of Commerce (12 commissioners) and the merchants and inhabitants of the town of Clonmel (five commissioners).[54] As highlighted above, the inclusion of representation from Waterford Corporation on the board of Waterford Harbour Commissioners came about as a late amendment to the bill following public lobbying and behind-the-scenes manoeuvring by the municipal authority. In the 18th and early 19th centuries, rather than reform national and urban government, parliament responded by creating new bodies with statutory powers, and often awarded these bodies greater powers than municipal authorities to borrow money and levy charges.[55] This tendency is reflected, in an Irish context, by the creation of the Wide Street Commissioners in Dublin in 1757, Cork in 1765 and Waterford in 1784,[56] along with the various harbour authorities detailed above.

Waterford Corporation, 'a bastion of Anglican privilege and exclusiveness',[57] was little different from most of the corporations of this era. Following the Act of Union, Waterford Corporation was one of 33 Irish municipal corporations empowered to return a total of 39 members to the parliament of Great Britain and Ireland,[58] ensuring that municipal politics interacted closely with parliamentary politics. In the early years of the 19th century, Waterford Corporation was dominated by a coterie of conservative Protestants led by William Congreve Alcock and Cornelius Bolton, while the liberal Protestant members of the corporation were steered by Sir John Newport.[59] These two sides fought bitterly to win the race for Waterford's single seat in parliament. In 1802, Sir John Newport was elected member of parliament for Waterford, defeating William Alcock,[60] and in 1807 Newport defeated his cousin Cornelius Bolton for the Waterford seat.[61] As discussed above, between 1818 and 1830, the unreformed corporation of Waterford was controlled by a secret compact between the Newport family and their opponents, the Alcocks.[62]

Of the seven politicians appointed to represent Waterford Corporation on Waterford Harbour Commissioners, two of them, Harry Alcock and James Wallace, would be signatories to the compact in 1818, and another commissioner, Michael Evelyn, would be one of the witnesses to the compact. Cornelius Bolton and Cornelius Henry Bolton were both conservative Protestants, who had established business ventures in Cheekpoint, Co. Waterford. The other two politicians appointed were Sir Nicholas Britiffe Skottowe and Edmund Skottowe, both members of Waterford Chamber of Commerce. Sir Nicholas sought to reconcile differences between the chamber and the corporation.[63]

The business interests and backgrounds of the commissioners appointed to represent Waterford Harbour Commissioners are outlined in Appendix 3. These men represented a diverse range of financial and commercial activities on which the city depended for its future. Included is Sir John Newport, who succeeded in having himself appointed a commissioner representing the chamber of commerce. Sir John appears in the chamber membership list for 1815 as 'merchant',[64] though he had retired from Newport's Bank to dedicate himself to politics.[65] A considerable number of the commissioners were Quakers, reflecting the significant Quaker membership of the chamber of commerce and the comparatively disproportionate involvement of the Quaker community in Irish industry.

The inclusion of the merchants and inhabitants of Clonmel, Co. Tipperary, on Waterford Harbour Commissioners is thought to have arisen at the insistence of the Bagwell family, an influential and wealthy Clonmel family, related to Sir John Newport, who threatened to oppose the bill if Clonmel interests were not protected.[66] Various members of the family represented Clonmel and Co. Tipperary in parliament. David Malcomson, one of the Clonmel merchants appointed to Waterford Harbour Commissioners, had connections to the family (Appendix 3).

The town of Clonmel sits on the northern banks of the Suir, 30 miles from Waterford. Originating in the medieval period, in the early 19th century it was a thriving market town, its prosperity built on its rich agricultural hinterland and its access to the navigable Suir.[67] There were over 20 corn mills in and around Clonmel in the early 19th century,[68] and it was the centre of Ireland's milling business, and most of the flour produced was exported through the port of Waterford.[69] The Quaker community were heavily represented in the merchant community in Clonmel, particularly in milling.[70] The trade of Clonmel depended on a navigable river connecting the town to the port and harbour of Waterford.

The bill for improving the port and harbour of Waterford had a somewhat tortuous passage through parliament. The intentions of Waterford Chamber of Commerce, under the guiding hand of the wily politician Sir John Newport, to try to achieve by legislation removal of the port and harbour from the rather dubious management of Waterford Corporation was thwarted by the municipal corporation, which challenged the proposed legislation and cleverly manoeuvred to have seven members of their corporate body appointed commissioners. The legislation enacted on 20 June 1816 set up a separate body to operate and manage the port under the guidance of 24 commissioners with varied, often conflicting interests and allegiances. Two of the bodies represented, Waterford Corporation and Waterford Chamber of Commerce, had been in conflict for years in relation to various aspects of port management. The merchants of Clonmel were added as commissioners for political reasons, and while the town in which they conducted their business was geographically removed from the port, the operation and development of the port and the navigation of the Suir were crucial to the future of the town. The profile of the commissioners representing both Waterford Chamber of Commerce and the merchant community of Clonmel reveals the extent of the spirit of Quaker entrepreneurism and business activism (Appendix 3). The members representing Waterford Chamber of Commerce on Waterford Harbour Commissioners had a personal stake in the future of the port, because either their own businesses, or the commercial interests of their families or social contacts depended on the viability of the port and city of Waterford. The Directors General of Inland Navigation in Ireland were appointed commissioners under the act in order that they might manage and supervise the works to be financed from the fund they managed. The next chapter will explore the manner in which this group of commissioners, with disparate aims and priorities, fulfilled the purpose of the act of 1816 charging them with responsibility for improving the port and harbour of Waterford.[71]

3. Shaping the port: implementing the act of 1816

The Waterford Harbour Act of 1816, for improving the port and harbour of Waterford, remained in place until the enactment on 27 July 1846 of an act for improving, preserving, maintaining and better regulating the port and harbour of Waterford.[1] This chapter will explore the performance of Waterford Harbour Commissioners from their establishment on 20 June 1816 until 1842 by looking at the manner in which the commissioners endeavoured to achieve the objectives of the act. It will first outline how the commissioners set about organizing the new port authority, examine the financial management of the authority, and then assess its impact on trade.

The first meeting of the newly appointed Waterford Harbour Commissioners was held on 17 July 1816, less than one month after the act came into force.[2] Of the 24 commissioners named in the 1816 act, 14 attended (table 5). While parliament had been adjourned until 24 August, Sir John Newport, who had worked tirelessly to ensure the establishment of Waterford Harbour Commissioners, was among those who did not attend the first meeting of the new body. Also absent were five of the members appointed to represent Waterford Corporation.

Table 5. Attendance at the first meeting of Waterford Harbour Commissioners[3]

	Waterford Corporation	Waterford Chamber of Commerce	Clonmel merchants
Present	Cornelius Bolton, James Wallace	John Harris, Richard Davis, Joseph Strangman, John Leonard, Robert Jacob, John Strangman, George Penrose Ridgway, Francis Davis	Arthur Riall, David Malcomson, James Morton, Robert Grubb
Absent	Harry Alcock, Michael Evelyn, Sir Nicholas Britiffe Skottowe, Edmund Skottowe, Cornelius Henry Bolton	Right Hon. Sir John Newport, Henry Holdsworth Hunt, Jeremiah Ryan, Edward Courtenay	Robert Banfield

The minutes of the first meeting do not record the venue for that meeting, but those present agreed to adjourn until the morning of Wednesday 31 July at the Chamber of Commerce building. What better way to demonstrate to the public the close links between the new body and the association of merchants

2. Waterford Chamber of Commerce building, George's Street, Waterford – the
headquarters of Waterford Harbour Commissioners from 1816 to 2004
(sketch by Eddie O'Keeffe)

who had played such a significant role in its creation than to meet in the imposing
Georgian building acquired so recently by the Chamber of Commerce as its
headquarters? On 31 July 1816, it was resolved that a committee be established
to seek a 'fit and proper place' with office accommodation for future meetings
of the commissioners.[4] The committee consisted of five commissioners, four
representing Waterford Chamber of Commerce and one presenting Waterford
Corporation,[5] and unsurprisingly on 28 August 1816 it was agreed that
Waterford Harbour Commissioners would rent three rooms, including the large
room to be fitted out as a ballast and pilot office, in the Chamber of Commerce
headquarters in George's Street, Waterford,[6] at an annual rent of £100.[7] The
establishment of a ballast office, as permitted under the act, created a monopoly
for the commissioners on the sale of this material, which was required to provide

stability when a vessel had little or no cargo. The act of 1816 empowered the commissioners to charge for ballast and specified the rates to be applied.[8]

In the early months of the new authority, the members met a number of times each month to put in place a structure and an organization that would enable it to fulfil its responsibilities under the 1816 act. They established a pilot, ballast, quay and finance committee to monitor, implement and control various aspects of the act. The new commissioners made several appointments to enable it to carry out its duties and functions, including the appointment of Henry Ivie, solicitor and member of Waterford Corporation, as its law agent.[9] George Brownrigg was appointed bookkeeper, a post later amalgamated with that of secretary, and James Lawson was appointed receiver of rates for the port.[10] Captain Thomas Hunt was appointed pilot master by Trinity House, having been recommended for the post by Sir John Newport and the members of the harbour commissioners on the basis that he was a 'careful, intelligent mariner' who had sailed from the port of Waterford 'for upward of 20 years in command of trading vessels', and Benjamin Conn was appointed as his deputy.[11] Trinity House appointed 19 pilots initially and on 1 November 1816 Benjamin Conn, deputy pilot master, brought these 19 men to the harbour commissioners offices in Waterford to receive their instructions.[12] In the following days a further 11 men were appointed pilots, bringing the total number of pilots to 30.[13]

Table 6. First pilots appointed under Waterford Harbour Act 1816

Name and age (years) of pilots appointed
Mat Barret (29), Bartly Barry (27), Thomas Barton (32), Mat Burke (24), Pat Burke (27), Martin Byrne (27), Thomas Carr (29), Val Connor (45), John Foran (24), Robert Fowler (24), James Kelly (40), Mick Kennedy (45), Thomas Kiely (40), James Harrington (47), John Henry (24), Edward Hogan (50), Richard Hogan (40), John Leg (28), Maurice Lyons (29), James Murray (40), John Murray (24), James Power (52), Richard Power (29), James Rack (25), Thomas Roche (41), Thomas Roger (39), Laurence Shanahan (30), Edward Toole (25), Edward Walsh (43), and Maurice Wyse (30).
Note: Michael Foran (50) 'declined the situation on account of having his boat'.[14]

The pilotage establishment began operating immediately and two days later in response to an order from Mr Courtenay, harbour commissioner, they succeeded in getting a vessel, the *Catherine* (under Captain Francis), off the rocks near Cromwell's Rock and mooring her safely on the graving bank.[15] The pilots' journals record many such rescues and a number of cases where, despite the efforts of all involved, lives and vessels were lost. On 8 March 1822, a brig, the *Martha*, laden with grain bound for Liverpool, upset in a squall and 'melancholy to relate all on board perished including the pilot James Power except the mate who swam until picked up by the pilot boat'.[16] Power was an experienced sailor aged 55, who had spent some 41 years at sea.[17] By the mid-1840s the number of pilots employed had increased to 33 with 10 assistant pilots.[18]

3. Seal of Waterford Harbour Commissioners reproduced with permission of Port of Waterford Company (photographed by Sheree Borge)

The commissioners resolved to commence by charging the full rate of tonnage duties permitted under the 1816 act (table 7), even though they were empowered to charge a lesser sum. They made this decision as they were aware that they would have to repay the loan to be advanced for the widening of the 'Ford'. The commissioners had given a public undertaking to reduce the rates by at least one half when the loan was repaid,[19] though it would be a couple of years before the commissioners were in a financial position to commence reducing the rate of tonnage duties.

Table 7. Tonnage duties to be charged on every vessel reporting to the Custom House of Waterford in accordance with Schedule A of the Act of 1816[20]

Vessel type	Amount of duty (stg.) per ton
Every vessel (vessels two-thirds of whose cargo shall be coals, or vessels arriving from any port in Ireland and foreign vessels excepted)	Not exceeding 6*d*.
Every vessel, two-thirds of whose cargo shall be coals	Not exceeding 4*d*.
Every vessel arriving from any port in Ireland	Not exceeding 3*d*.
Every vessel of every kind of any other nation or country except those of the United Kingdom of Great Britain and Ireland, and the Colonies, Islands, and possessions thereunto belonging	Double the rates chargeable on British and Irish vessels

While the corporation and the commissioners felt confident that they had resolved the issue of the water bailiff's fees, the new body were forced to re-evaluate the issue soon after its establishment. The corporation's Law Agent, Charles Samuel Tandy, submitted a draft lease to the commissioners in compliance with the terms of the agreement of 15 May 1816.[21] The commissioners referred the lease to legal counsel in Dublin.[22] It appears that legal counsel raised concerns regarding the proposal contained in the agreement of 15 May 1816 – namely that the commissioners would lease from the corporation, in perpetuity, the water bailiff's place, and all the powers and duties of the office – as a further agreement was entered into between Waterford Corporation and Waterford Harbour Commissioners on 28 October 1816 to the effect that:

> Until an act of parliament can be procured, the best mode of carrying the above agreement into effect will be that the corporation should agree to appoint such persons that the commissioners may from time to time nominate as deputy water bailiff, the commissioners indemnifying the water bailiff appointed by the corporation from any and every illegal act committed by the said deputy, the commissioners undertaking to pay the water bailiffs appointed by the corporation £400 p.a. in quarterly payments, the corporation undertaking to support the commissioners in the collection of duties and fees.[23]

No act of parliament in the 19th century changed this situation and no lease was completed.[24] In effect, the corporation appointed two water bailiffs who were rarely called on to perform any tasks, the work being carried out by the deputy water bailiffs nominated by Waterford Harbour Commissioners.[25] Michael Evelyn and Simon Newport, supporters of Sir John Newport, were appointed water bailiffs under the Newport/Alcock compact of 1818.[26] When Simon Newport died in 1832, the salary that had been paid to him (£200 p.a.) was then paid by the Harbour Commissioners to the corporation and became part of the borough fund.[27] It appears that the corporation's determination to retain the post of water bailiff was motivated by a desire to have the rewarding of the post within its gift. Evelyn confirmed that since the appointment of deputy water bailiffs nominated by the commissioners, the entire duties of the post were carried out by these deputies at a salary of £50 p.a., the office of water bailiff being now 'a mere sinecure'.[28]

Waterford Harbour Commissioners appointed William Newport & Co. as their treasurer and received an advance of £1,000 from the bank to enable them to function until they had operated long enough to realize income from the various charges the act of 1816 empowered them to levy.[29] The decision to appoint this bank as treasurer by the first statutory board of harbour commissioners for Waterford may have been influenced by a sense of loyalty to the family business of Sir John Newport, a man closely involved in the establishment of the new authority, but the decision most likely reflected the fact that Newport's Bank was the chief bank in the city in this period.[30] When the bank collapsed in 1820,[31] Waterford Harbour Commissioners was one of the many organizations and businesses affected by the collapse of a trusted institution whose 'stoppage ruined many'.[32] At the date on which the bank became insolvent, 6 June 1820, the commissioners held monies to the value of £3,956 8s. 9d. in the bank, and the commissioners, like many other creditors, lodged a claim on the estate.[33] During the year ending 5 January 1822, the assignees of William Newport & Co., paid a dividend of 6s. 8d. in the pound to its creditors. Waterford Harbour Commissioners were recompensed to the value of £1,318 16s. 3d. in that year,[34] and they received further dividends in the years ending 5 January 1823, 1825, and 1831.[35] The final loss borne by the commissioners from the collapse of Newport's Bank amounted to approximately £1,800.[36]

The main sources of income to fund the operation of Waterford Harbour Commissioners came from tonnage duty payable by each vessel reporting at the Custom House in Waterford city; ballast duty payable in respect of the making available of solid material to provide stability when a vessel had little or no cargo and pilotage duties payable in respect of the provision of pilots familiar with the obstacles and tides of the harbour who were appointed to pilot vessels through the harbour.[37] The pilot stations were established at Passage East and Dunmore East. Each vessel was boarded by the deputy pilot master or his assistant and details of the tonnage, draught of water, cargo and destination of each vessel were recorded and forwarded daily to the ballast office for calculation of duties.[38]

Rates of tonnage duties charged to the owners of vessels was reduced over the years in accordance with the undertaking given by the commissioners to reduce the rates set in the 1816 act as soon as they were in a financial position to do so.[39] The rates were halved with effect from 29 September 1818,[40] and reduced by a further one halfpenny per ton from 5 April 1824.[41] This allowed Waterford to compete more favourably with its nearest competitor, the port of Cork, where an act passed in 1820 set the following tonnage rates for that port:

Table 8. Tonnage rates in the port of Cork under the 1820 act[42]

Vessel type	*Amount of duty (stg.) per ton*
Every vessel (excl. colliers & coasters)	Not exceeding 3d.
Colliers (coal carrying vessels)	Not exceeding 2d.
Coasters from any port in Ireland	Not exceeding 1d.

The accounts of Waterford Harbour Commissioners were subject to forensic annual audit by the Commissioners for Public Audit, and this body had the power to disallow sums charged to the account. The main items of recurring expenditure incurred by the commissioners related to salaries and wages, rent to the chamber of commerce, lighterage costs for transferring cargo from vessels in order to achieve the level of draft to permit entry to the port, boats for the pilot operation, rents on watch houses in Passage East and Dunmore East for the pilots, pensions, office provisions, and legal expenses. The annual income and expenditure data for Waterford Harbour Commissioners for the period 1816 to 31 March 1837 is set out below. At the end of that period the accounts were in credit to the sum of £ 868 2s. 6d. (stg.) but on a year by year basis, expenditure was beginning to outstrip income.[43]

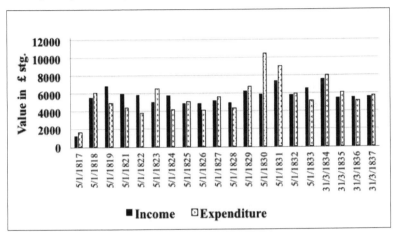

4. Income and expenditure of Waterford Harbour Commissioners, 1816–37[44]

The commissioners worked within the somewhat narrow income stream available to them under the act and managed their resources so as to maintain their accounts in credit, unlike Drogheda Harbour Commissioners, to which a receiver was appointed by the Office of Public Works in 1840.[45] The commissioners funded a number of projects to improve the quays, erect hulks and further deepen the channel. The 'installation of hulks' referred to below relate to a system developed to deal with the tendency for mud to build up alongside the quayside in Waterford, whereby a series of bridges or gangways were erected, with one side of each bridge or gangway resting on the quay, and the other on a floating hulk.[46] Vessels mooring in Waterford to receive or discharge cargo or passengers tied up at these hulks or stages, which had the advantage that the deck of the vessel was at all times level with the deck of the floating hulk.[47] These hulks or jetties are visible on the 1842 6-inch Ordnance Survey map.

Table 9. Examples of monies expended by Waterford Harbour Commissioners on improvement works at the inner area of Waterford port and harbour between 1817 and 1838

Year ended	Details	Cost £	s.	d.
5 Jan 1818[48]	Expenses of quays	668	12	5
5 Jan 1821[49]	Repairing the quays	52	14	1
5 Jan 1823[50]	Expenses of the river Suir	1,462	6	1
	Expenses of quays and docks	1,004	6	–
5 Jan 1824[51]	Expenses of quays	258	12	2
5 Jan 1829[52]	Expenses of works at river Suir	130	4	5
	Expenses of works at quays	1,497	2	8
	Expenses of works at hulk, British Isle	305	9	10
5 Jan 1830[53]	Expenses of works at the river Suir	4,118	19	8
	Quay and river moorings	48	19	8
	Hulks, gangways and wharf	1,164	4	4
	Quays and steps	1,238	15	1
5 Jan 1831[54]	Expenses of the river Suir	443	19	2
	Hulks and gangways	414	13	10
	Quays, steps and wharfs	1,960	6	10
5 Jan 1832[55]	Expenses of the river Suir	647	14	9½
	Moorings, buoys and perches	31	5	–
	Hulks and gangways	609	18	6
	Quays, steps and wharfs	538	17	8
5 Jan 1833[56]	Expenses of the river Suir – for mud raised and	183	16	1
	landed and for changes connected with Upper and	526	12	6
	Lower Ford			
	Hulks and gangways	147	5	5
6 Jan 1833 to	River and quay moorings	398	13	11
31 Mar 1834[57]	Hulks and gangways	485	14	09
	Quay, piers, slips and steps	1,838	19	11
31 Mar 1837[58]	Hulks and gangways	1,029	14	11
31 Mar 1838[59]	Hulks and gangways	1,865	2	0
	Quay, piers, slips and steps	941	19	11

Some of the works carried out by Waterford Harbour Commissioners were partially funded by Waterford Corporation under an agreement entered into by both bodies.[60] In the audit of the accounts of Waterford Harbour Commissioners in the years ending 5 January 1820 and 1821, the Commissioners for Auditing Public Accounts in Ireland disallowed monies to the value of £166 1s. 4d. included in the accounts by the harbour commissioners in respect of monies expended on repairing the quays in Waterford.[61] The harbour commissioners defended the expenditure on the basis that repair of the quays was one of the original objectives of the act, and that they could not comprehend 'any object more inseparably connected with, and essential to the improvement of the Port and Harbour of Waterford, than building and repairing the quays'.[62] However, five members of the harbour commissioners, four of whom represented Clonmel, objected to carrying out works on infrastructure owned by Waterford Corporation.[63] Having taken advice from the attorney general that the works to the quays were within the limits of the act of 1816, the public accounts commission allowed the expenditure.[64] Under the agreement entered into in the year ended 5 January 1823, Waterford Corporation paid the commissioners the sum of £613 7s. 9d. in the year ending 5 January 1824, representing half the cost of the new quay erected between the Market House and the Fish House,[65] and in the year ending 5 January 1829, the corporation paid over the sum of £590 1s. ½d., accounting for half the cost of the erection of a stone quay and two flights of steps at 'the Scotch Pill'.[66]

As stated, under the terms of the Waterford Harbour Act 1816, the Irish Treasury was empowered to advance a loan, not exceeding £10,000, out of the consolidated fund for Ireland for the purposes of 'deepening, cleaning and improving' the river Suir at the port and harbour of Waterford in order to 'promote the trade and commerce' of Waterford.[67] The loan was to be advanced to the Directors General of Inland Navigation in Ireland and the harbour commissioners. While the necessary works were being planned and built, sole responsibility for their management and that of all expenditure relating to the project rested with the Directors General, with the commissioners debarred from any interference or control.[68] When the works were completed, they were to be vested in and come under the commissioners' control and management.[69]

The Directors General did not attend meetings of Waterford Harbour Commissioners. Immediately prior to the first meeting of the commissioners, they sought details of the petition submitted to parliament by Waterford Chamber of Commerce, and Cornelius Bolton was instructed to prepare the necessary reply.[70] This petition had sought funding for improvements consisting of the removal of natural impediments in the direct river channel to the city, at a place called the 'Ford', and the creation of a new direct channel that would permit vessels to navigate directly to the quays in Waterford.[71] On 19 December 1816, the Directors General of Inland Navigation entered into a contract of 18 months duration, commencing on 1 May 1817, with John Hughes of London for the excavation of the 'shoal called the ford in the river Suir' at a cost of stg £14,500.[72] On 28 August 1817, the dredging vessel for deepening the Ford arrived, having being towed from Dungarvan by the boats of the pilot establishment assisted by Francis Davis.[73]

The total cost of the works to enlarge and deepen the Ford north of Little Island and thereby create a direct route for vessels to the quays in Waterford, enabled by the act of 1816 was in the region of £24,588.[74] The exchequer advances are set out in table 10. When completed in the late 1820s, the width of the cut was 70 yards, with a depth of seven feet at low tide and a depth of 20 feet at high-water spring tides.[75] With the exception of works to the quays, and the erection of hulks and jetties, no further significant works were carried out by the commissioners in the inner harbour in the period under consideration.

The exchequer funding from the grant of £500,000 issued to the Directors General of Inland Navigation in Ireland, which exceeded the original proposed advance of £10,000, made available for the works approved under the act of 1816 was as follows:

Table 10. Monies applied by the Directors General of Inland Navigation in Ireland on river Suir navigation under the 1816 act for improvements to Waterford port and harbour[76]

Year	Source of funding	Application of funding	Amount £ s. d.		
1816	£500,000 grant from public funds advanced to the Directors in 1800	Suir navigation	30	17	9¼
1817	Ditto	Ditto	5,060	1	2¾
1818	Ditto	Ditto	3,942	19	8¾
1819	Ditto	Ditto	3,132	12	6
1820	Ditto	Ditto	2,269	13	2½
1821	Ditto	Ditto	2,054	9	8¼
		TOTAL	16,490	14	0

The commissioners felt constrained by the narrow remit of the act of 1816, as is evident from a petition they submitted to parliament on 15 February 1830 seeking amendments to the act.[77] This petition arose from a unanimous decision of the commissioners at a meeting held on 19 November 1829 that alterations were required to the pilotage system, which was considered unsatisfactory.[78] Under the 1816 act pilots were paid a fixed annual salary, whereas in many of the other ports in Ireland, pilots were recompensed by receiving a certain portion of the pilotage fees payable by the vessel owners. The commissioners felt that such a payment system encouraged the 'zeal and activity' of the pilots.[79] The petition, as submitted, cited the fact that the provisions of the act were defective and insufficient and hampered the commissioners' ability to manage and operate the pilot establishment formed under the direction of Trinity House and to control and direct the berthing of vessels in the harbour without the aid of the corporation-appointed water bailiff. Consequently, the act needed to be amended to give legal effect to the agreement entered into with Waterford Corporation on that matter. In addition, the commissioners stated that they had recently put in place a quay and river watch system that had saved lives and prevented pilfering; however, the act did not give the commissioners the authority to collect and apply the fees from ships' masters necessary to operate this watch system.[80]

Parliament resolved that Sir John Newport and Thomas Spring Rice prepare a draft bill.[81] It has not been possible to ascertain the extent to which the draft bill that emerged reflected the contents of the draft bill prepared by the Pilot Committee and the harbour commissioners' law agent and referred to in the minutes of the harbour commissioners dated 19 November 1829. The draft bill that emerged from parliament contained provisions that were found repugnant by various individual and bodies.[82]

A public meeting was held in City Hall on 29 March 1830 to consider the bill before the house of commons.[83] The meeting was called by the mayor, following receipt of a request by a number of 'the most respectable of citizens'.[84] Richard Fogarty, a Catholic merchant, objected to the proposal in the bill to reduce, to an unspecified number the number of members required to adopt bye-laws under that act, and also the proposal to reduce the number of commissioners from the 24 provided for under the act of 1816 to an unspecified number.[85] Fogarty was active in the Catholic Association,[86] and was a member of the Waterford Liberal Club, founded in July 1828 by Thomas Wyse, a club that strove to achieve the right for Catholic participation in corporation and parliamentary politics.[87] Fogarty argued that the number of harbour commissioners should be increased, as it would be unfair for a small board to control income averaging £6,000 a year. Additionally, he claimed that the chamber of commerce, due to reduced membership, was finding it difficult to provide sufficient members to fulfil its requirements under the act.[88] This is supported by the fact that on occasion meetings had to be adjourned due to the failure of sufficient members to attend. He proposed that the number of members should be increased by between eight and 12 members, to be selected publicly from the merchants and traders rather than from the ranks of Waterford Corporation and Waterford Chamber of Commerce.[89] This proposal was supported by Thomas Wyse, Catholic merchant and landowner, and others present. A committee was established representing the corporation, the chamber of commerce and the merchants, traders and ship owners, to discuss the proposed bill.

The proposal to extend the membership of the harbour commissioners beyond the groupings set down in the act of 1816 may have been influenced by the fact that Drogheda's Catholic merchants had succeeded in 1827 in obtaining an act of parliament that removed the exclusive power of the corporation to nominate harbour commissioners in favour of a new membership qualification based on property and wealth.[90] This proposal for changes to the composition of Waterford Harbour Commissioners, which, if successful, would have opened membership to Catholic merchants, was a sign of the growing confidence of Waterford's Catholics. This burgeoning assertiveness became a source of concern even for liberal Protestants.[91] When this proposal to extend membership of Waterford Harbour Commissioners beyond the provisions contained in the act of 1816 was reported to a meeting of the harbour commissioners, it was found to be totally unacceptable to the board of commissioners who, past grievances put aside, were unanimous in their opinion that the number of commissioners established under the existing act were 'fully sufficient' for the purposes of the act and refused to accede to the proposition that persons outside the ranks of the corporation and the chamber be admitted.[92] Copies of the amended draft bill were forwarded to the Chamber of Commerce and the Commercial Association of Clonmel for consideration.[93] The commissioners made alterations to the draft bill and forwarded same to Sir John Newport, with instructions that in the event that attempts were made to introduce any further alterations to the draft bill without the sanction of the commissioners, that he 'will be pleased to withdraw' the bill for the present session.[94]

The joint committee appointed at the public meeting of 29 March, met on three occasions in April, and expressed objections to a significant number of provisions of the draft bill relating, inter alia, to the proposal to reduce the number of members required to pass bye-laws from 13 to 10, certain changes to the pilotage structure, proposals to fine masters of vessels and arrangements relating to the water bailiff, reporting to a public meeting their recommendations that significant provisions of the bill be expunged.[95] The joint committee representing the corporation, chamber and merchants concurred on many issues, however the committee appointed to represent the merchants, traders and shipowners were firmly of the opinion that the discharge of their duties were too arduous for the present limited number of harbour commissioners, a fact they considered the commissioners concurred with as they were proposing to reduce the number of members necessary to pass bye-laws.[96] The committee considered that the decline in the membership of Waterford Chamber of Commerce, from 120 members when the 1816 act was adopted, to 42 at present, meant that the chamber no longer fairly represented the merchant community, and consequently they recommended that an additional five members be appointed to the board of Waterford Harbour Commissioners to represent the 'large and respectable body of merchants, traders and ship-owners of this city, not members of the corporation and chamber of commerce'.[97] When the report reflecting the deliberations of the joint committee were read at a meeting held on Monday 3 May 1830, it was resolved that the further progress of the bill should be stopped and Sir John Newport be notified of this decision.[98] On 7 May 1830, Sir John Newport wrote to the mayor confirming that having received the resolutions of the citizens from this meeting he had signified to parliament his refusal to 'take any further part in the proceedings, which of course closes the proceedings in the measure'.[99] It would be another sixteen years before the act of 1816 would be overhauled.

By 1838, the volume of mud accumulated at the quayside in Waterford had grown considerably as the natural configuration of the river and the nature of the tides occurring combined to cause the deposition of mud in this location, a situation that had been exacerbated by the increased volume of shipping activity in the port.[100] The commissioners sought a report on the state of the quays from civil engineer William Cubitt,[101] who recommended that the most economical means of dealing with the issue was to employ a quality dredging machine, and a number of barges, at an outlay of approximately £5,000.[102] A dredging machine was commissioned from Malcomson's Neptune Ironworks in Waterford and this machine began work dredging mud in the river in 1844, though it proved inefficient initially due to design issues.[103] The 1846 report of the Tidal Harbour Commissioners confirmed that, at Waterford, an 'extensive mudbank still lines the foot of the finest range of quays in the United Kingdom'.[104]

The purpose of the act of 1816 was to fund improvements to the port and harbour of Waterford so as to 'promote the trade and commerce of the said city',[105] and there was a significant increase in activity in the port during the period under consideration. The Pilot Book records that on 9 February 1838 'a fleet of vessels (in number ninety sail) the largest recorded since the formation of this establishment sailed this day'.[106] The amount of the combined tonnage entering inwards and clearing outwards of the port of Waterford in 1819 was 141,560 tons, carried in 1,419 ships,[107] which increased by 1841 to 338,995 tons in 3,190 ships.[108] Waterford retained its position as the fourth-busiest port in Ireland, after Belfast, Dublin and Cork.

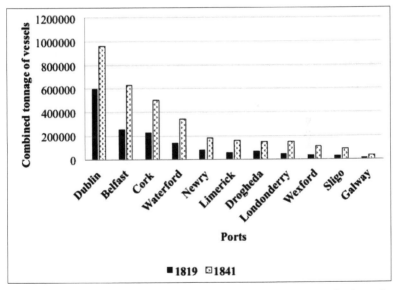

5. The combined tonnage of vessels entering inwards and clearing outwards of several ports in Ireland in 1819[109] and 1841[110]

A further measure of the commercial activity and financial confidence of a port is the amount of ships belonging to and registered at the port. An unusual feature of the port of Waterford was the extent to which merchants and traders relied on British vessels to transport their produce and cargos.[111] Likewise, the corporation, as port authority, did not provide dry docks and repair facilities. Shortly after the commencement of the act of 1816 which established Waterford Harbour Commissioners, a Quaker, Thomas White, commenced the construction of a dockyard and slipway on the north side of the river at Ferrybank.[112] The first ship was built here in 1820, and the business thrived in the following decades, building steam vessels from 1837. However, Waterford lagged far behind Dublin, Belfast and Cork. Cork became the main ship-building centre in Ireland in the 1820s and 1830s.[113] Another Quaker family, that of Harbour Commissioner David Malcomson, was planning an expansion into shipping and shipbuilding in Waterford in 1842 and opened Neptune Ironworks in February 1843.[114] The navigation of the river Suir and the availability of affordable and efficient river transport was vital to the Malcomson enterprises at Clonmel, Co. Tipperary and at Pouldrew and Portlaw, Co. Waterford. Consequently, it has been claimed that the Malcomson family 'single-handedly provided the most significant economic boost of the 19th century to the Suir Valley region'.[115] These factors, together with increases in trade, may have given Waterford merchants the confidence to invest in ship ownership, and from 1835 Waterford experienced a growth in the number and tonnage of ships registered and belonging to the port (table 11).

Table 11. Number and tonnage of vessels registered at the main ports in Ireland

Port	1831[116]		1835[117]		1842[118]	
	Ships	*Tonnage*	*Ships*	*Tonnage*	*Ships*	*Tonnage*
Belfast	251	25,453	281	30,259	370	50,514
Dublin	280	22,501	299	23,412	388	33,364
Cork	258	16,510	298	20,640	367	34,542
Waterford	**81**	**8,085**	**115**	**11,986**	**171**	**20,137**
Newry	161	7,761	150	7,577	209	10,825
Wexford	135	6,968	111	6,842	110	8,728
Londonderry	31	4,314	42	5,677	34	8,786
Limerick	47	2,060	64	4,149	116	14,742
Drogheda	31	2,396	40	3,763	45	6,650
Sligo	17	1,140	16	1,476	37	4,363
Galway	18	894	7	272	21	2,888

Of the ships registered in Waterford port in 1842, four steam ships are included, with six steam ships registered in Belfast, five in Drogheda, two in Cork and 45 in Dublin in the same period.[119] The emergence of steam transport had a significant economic effect in the 1820s. The first steam service, the P.S. *Ivanhoe*, plying the route between Milford Haven and Dunmore East, was introduced in

6. View of Waterford in the 1830s by W.H. Bartlett – print in possession of author.

1824.[120] In anticipation of steam trade, the Harbour Commissioners built new berthage on the quays.[121] The *Nora Crevin*, a paddle steamer, was purchased by local businessmen, who established the Waterford and Bristol Steam Navigation Company, and operated a thrice-weekly system of journeys between the two cities.[122]

The minutes of the general proceedings of Waterford Harbour Commissioners are very matter-of-fact, meticulously maintained records of resolutions and decisions of the commissioners. However, they lack detail and contain little to illuminate the relationships among the various commissioners or the bodies they represented or the background discussions and debate that informed their decisions. The commission established to enquire into Irish municipal corporations in 1833 interviewed persons involved in all the statutory bodies in the city and reported that 'it was suggested' that as the Harbour Commissioners, who had control over significant funds, were elected by three self-selecting bodies, Waterford Chamber of Commerce, Waterford Corporation and the merchants of Clonmel, it would be right to give the public a say in the appointment of commissioners, and also that membership should be confined to persons connected with the shipping, trade and commerce of the city.[123] This suggests that the merchants still desired total control over the operation of the maritime authority and many excluded by religion or wealth desired representation on the harbour board. In 1830, when faced with a proposition that

7 Map of Waterford, 1834 (extract showing quays and inner port) by Patrick Leahy – reproduced with permission of Waterford City and County Archives.

persons outside the echelons of the corporation and the merchant body be eligible for membership of Waterford Harbour Commissioners, the commissioners closed ranks. The harbour commissioners appear to have sacrificed alterations to the act of 1816 they considered worthwhile and necessary in order to protect their status and avoid the imposition of provisions they considered repugnant. The draft bill containing these objectionable provisions was drawn up by Sir John Newport and Sir Thomas Spring Rice and the purpose and motivation for these proposed alterations to the 1816 act deserve further research.

Nevertheless, the various interests represented on Waterford Harbour Commissioners worked together in the period 1816 to 1842 to improve the port and harbour of Waterford. The agreement entered into in 1821 whereby the corporation agreed to contribute, from time to time, towards the cost of works, not exceeding £1,500, at the quays, was instigated by the corporation.[124] The harbour commissioners recorded that they found this agreement to be both 'unexpected and highly advantageous to the public' and acknowledged that there was no legal obligation on the corporation to fund this work.[125] The commissioners built new quays, increased berthage, developed a system of floating jetties and hulks suitable to the unique riverine and tidal circumstances (a system that met with the approval of William Cubitt, a respected civil engineer and vice-president of the Institute of Civil Engineers),[126] erected buoys at various locations along the harbour to aid navigation, entered into an agreement with the Waterford Gas Company in 1830 to have 13 gas lights erected at the edge of the quays, adopted bye-laws to implement and regulate the various purposes of the 1816 act, and cooperated with Trinity House to appoint pilots and erect lights at several locations including at Duncannon and Hook Head. In addition, the commissioners remained solvent, unlike their counterparts in Drogheda, who were placed in receivership,[127] and the Cork commissioners, who were forced to issue debentures.[128]

There were increases in the number of ships and tonnage through the port of Waterford and the number and tonnage of vessels registered and belonging to the port. In the decades before the Famine, Waterford retained its position as the fourth port in Ireland but failed to make any appreciable improvement to gain on its competitor ports. As it entered into the 1840s it faced many challenges, including physical and structural shortcomings in the port and harbour, the impending impact of the Municipal Corporations Act 1840 which would change the composition of municipal authorities, and the unforeseen and devastating Great Famine.

Conclusion

Waterford port and harbour has been central to the fortunes of the city and its hinterland, bringing friend and foe alike to the area, and providing a conduit for the importation of necessities and the exportation of goods vital for the survival of an export-reliant economy.

This short book has explored the port and harbour of Waterford in the period from 1815 to 1842 through the lens of the political and mercantile elites who had a vested interest in the management and development of the port and harbour. Waterford Harbour Commissioners established in 1816, along with Waterford Corporation, masters of the port and harbour under the charter of 1626, and Waterford Chamber of Commerce, the body representing the merchants and traders, each played significant roles.

Waterford and other Irish ports were at the heart of Ireland's export-oriented economy. Despite the challenges and competition facing Waterford port in 1815, the Chamber of Commerce, emboldened by the award of a royal charter, utilized the complex relationship between the local MP, Sir John Newport, and the commercial interests in the municipal borough to drive through a local act that would considerably dilute the municipal corporation's control over the port. A foretaste of the weaknesses, corruption and abuses of power that would emerge in the 1835 report of the commissioners charged with enquiring into the municipal corporations in Ireland was revealed in the claims of the chamber of commerce relating to the corporation's management of the port.

The resolute efforts of Waterford Corporation to retain their 'ancient privileges' over the port is representative of the attempts of early 19th-century municipal corporations to reflexively resist any challenges that would herald reform and endanger their position as strongholds of Protestant privilege. The lack of uniformity in the various parliamentary acts setting up harbour authorities demonstrates central government's failure to grapple with reform of local government, resulting in the creation of a plethora of self-electing bodies with greater funding powers than the municipal authorities. The profile of the members of the newly appointed Waterford Harbour Commissioners, and the membership lists of Waterford Chamber of Commerce shine a light on the nature of, and participation in, early 19th-century trade and commerce in Waterford city, demonstrating in particular the importance of Quaker entrepreneurship to the industrial and mercantile development of Waterford and its hinterland.

The manner in which Waterford Harbour Commissioners carried out its responsibilities in relation to the management and development of Waterford port and harbour from establishment in 1816 to 1842 reveals a body that was cautious and fiscally prudent. The major portion of the capital monies expended on improving the port and inner harbour area in the period was approved and managed by a group of men who were commissioners in name only and never attended meetings – the Directors General of Inland Navigation in Ireland.

Like their predecessors, Waterford Corporation, the Waterford Harbour Commissioners were determined to securely retain the management of the port in the hands of their own elite group. They fought off a proposal that would have opened membership to wealthy Catholic merchants and, with the support of Sir John Newport and Waterford Corporation, they ensured that a bill instigated at the request of the harbour commissioners, but found to contain provisions that they found unacceptable, failed. The trade and commerce of the port improved under their stewardship, with the number of vessels registered at the port more than doubling in the final 10 years of this study and the combined tonnage entering inwards and clearing outwards of the port of Waterford increasing from 141,560 tons in 1819 to 338,995 tons 1841.[1] In this period Waterford retained its position as the fourth-busiest Irish port.

The decisions as to how the port and harbour were to develop and the management of their day-to-day operation were in the hands of an elite group from which most citizens, and many merchants and traders, were excluded by virtue of religion and financial circumstances. The body set up to replace Waterford Corporation was another self-electing body, in which the corporation had representation and influence, and the new body guarded its position and privileges as closely as had the old. Waterford port and harbour between 1815 and 1842 evolved in a milieu where political and civic positions were the preserve of the Protestant elite. However, it was also a society in transition, with Catholics succeeding in mercantile and industrial enterprises, becoming increasingly confident and demanding a right to a role in politics and civic institutions.

Membership of Waterford Chamber of Commerce in 1815[1]

William A. Ardagh (brewer), William Aylward (merchant), Henry A. Bayly (merchant), William Belcher (flour and spirit merchant), Arthur Birnie (bookseller), Andrew Blain (merchant), William Blain (merchant), James Blake (merchant and shipowner), Thomas Boland (merchant), Richard Cherry (R. & W. Cherry, brewers and insurance), William Cherry (R. & W. Cherry, brewers and insurance), Edward Courtenay (merchant), Francis Davis, Richard Davis (Davis & Son, brewers), Richard Davis Jnr. (Davis & Son, brewers), Samuel S. Davis (Davis & Son., timber merchants), Henry Downes, Maurice Farrell (M., P. & M. Farrell, merchants and shipbrokers), Joseph Fayle (Scott, Fayle, merchants and boot manufacturers), Samuel W. Fayle (merchant and boot manufacturer), Richard Fogarty (merchant), Jonathan Gatchell (merchant and glass manufacturer), Peter Gibbons, James Harris (banker), John Harris (Wm. & John Harris, merchants), William Harris (Wm. & John Harris, merchants, and insurance agent), James Hill (flour merchant), William Hughes (excise collector), Henry H. Hunt (Hunt, O'Brien & Hunt, merchants and bankers), Robert Hunt (Hunt, O'Brien & Hunt, merchants and bankers), William Hunt (Hunt, O'Brien & Hunt, merchants and bankers), Thomas Hutchinson (McCheane & Hutchinson, merchants), Anthony Jackson (merchant), Isaac Jacob, Joseph Jacob (T.R. & J. Jacob, timber merchants), Joshua Jacob (merchant and ironmonger), Joshua R. Jacob (merchant), Robert Jacob (T.R. & J. Jacob, timber merchants), Thomas Jacob (T.R. & J. Jacob, timber merchants), David Jones (King & Jones, timber merchants), Alderman S. King (King & Jones, timber merchants), Joseph A. Leonard (merchant), John Leonard (merchant), William Leonard (merchant), Joshua Mason (merchant, tallow chandler and insurance co.), Simon Max (merchant), Thomas McCheane (McCheane & Hutchinson, merchants), George Milward, William Milward, Phineas Murphy (wine merchant), Penrose Nevins (T. Nevins, Pim & Penrose, merchants), Thomas Nevins (T. Nevins, Pim & Penrose, merchants), Pim Nevins (T. Nevins, Pim & Penrose, merchants), Sir J. Newport Bart (merchant), Alderman William Newport (Newport & Scott, bankers), Joshua Newsom, Joshua Peet (Edward Peet & Son, merchants), William Peet (Edward Peet & Son, merchants), Francis Penrose (F. Penrose & Co., timber merchant and shipping), John Penrose, William Penrose, Alexander Pope (lawyer and notary public), Richard Pope (merchant and ship broker), Thomas

Prosser (merchant), Henry Ridgway (Ridgeway & Sons, butter merchants), George P. Ridgway (Ridgeway & Sons, butter merchants), Henry Ridgway, Jnr. (Ridgeway & Sons, butter merchants), William Robinson (spirit and corn factor), Jeremiah Ryan (wine merchant), Thomas Scott (Newport & Scott, bankers), Jacob Scroder (commission agent), Edmund Skottowe (merchant), Nicholas Skottowe (Atkinson, Skottowe & Roberts, bankers), Francis Smith, John Strangman, Joseph Strangman (merchant), Joshua Strangman (merchant), Joshua Strangman, Jnr., William Strangman (brewer and merchant), Charles Trouton, Matthew J. Turner, Joseph Wakefield (Procter & Wakefield, merchants and ironmongers), Robert Watson, William Penrose Watson, Samuel White (boot and shoe manufacturer), Thomas White (Russia merchant and wholesale grocer), and William White (merchant, rope and ship manufacturer).

Agreements entered into between Waterford Corporation and Waterford Harbour Commissioners regarding the water bailiff

IST AGREEMENT DATED I5 SEPTEMBER I8I6.

WHEREAS a bill is now depending before the Parliament of the United Kingdom for the improvement of the port and harbour of Waterford whereby it is intended that we the undersigned shall with certain other persons in said bill named be appointed Commissioners for certain purposes in said Act mentioned **AND WHEREAS** it was agreed on between the Commissioners in the said Bill named and the Corporation of the city of Waterford that all the powers and fees of the Water Bailiff should be vested in the said Commissioners in consideration whereof said Commissioners should for ever hereafter pay to the said Corporation the annual sum of four hundred pounds by half yearly payments and **WHEREAS** it has been since suggested that the beforementioned agreement may create difficulties to the passing of the said bill and it has been therefore agreed upon between us the undersigned on the one part and the Corporation of Waterford on the other part that all those ~~claims~~ clauses which relate to the powers & fees of the Water Bailiff together with the schedule of the Water Bailiffs fees shall be expunged from the said bill altogether and that a saving of the Water Bailiffs rights and powers be introduced into the said Bill in lieu thereof and that immediately on the said bill being enacted into a law the Commissioners in said bill named shall take a lease of the Water Bailiffs place with all the fees and powers thereto appertaining as in the draft of the said Bill mentioned, from the Corporation of Waterford **To hold** to said Commissioners and their successors for ever at the yearly rent of four hundred pounds payable half yearly on every 25th March and 29th September subject to all the conditions in the draft of said Bill mentioned and which lease the said Corporation do hereby bind themselves and their successors to grant **In Witness** thereof we the undersigned persons have signed this Memorandum this 15 May 1816

Signed: Cornelius Bolton, N.B. Skottowe, Edm Skottowe, John Strangman, John Harris.

2ND AGREEMENT DATED 28 OCTOBER 1816

It was agreed that for the present and until an Act of parliament can be procured, the best mode of carrying the above agreement into effect will be, that the Corporation should agree to appoint such persons as the Commissioners may from time to time nominate as Deputy Water bailiff, the Commissioners indemnifying the Water Bailiff appointed by the Corporation against any and every illegal act committed by the said deputy. The Commissioners undertake to pay the Water Bailiffs appointed by the Corporation four hundred pounds per annum in quarterly payments, the Corporation undertaking to support the Commissioners in the collection of duties and fees attached to the Water Bailiff's office agreeable to the Schedule already furnished.

The office to be taken possession of by the deputy nominated by the Commissioners on 25th December next and the payment of the four hundred pounds per annum to commence from that day. It was further agreed that these proceedings should be entered on the books of the Corporation and the Commissioners for improving the Harbour and be considered binding on both bodies.

Signed on the part of the Corporation: Hen. Sargint, James Hackett, John Perkins.
Signed on the part of the Commissioners: Henry H. Hunt, John Harris.

Profile of the First Board of Harbour Commissioners

WATERFORD CORPORATION

HARRY ALCOCK of Wilton, Co. Wexford, succeeded to the estate of his older brother, William Congreve Alcock in 1813.[1] He was an alderman on the corporation and served as mayor of Waterford city in 1815/16.[2]

CORNELIUS BOLTON (1746–1829), of Faithlegg, Co. Waterford, was the grandson of Henry Bolton and Elizabeth Alcock, daughter of Benjamin Alcock, and son of Cornelius Bolton and Frances Barker.[3] He followed in his father's footsteps and served as MP from 1778 to 1783. However, he was defeated by his cousin Sir John Newport in 1807. The Boltons were improving landlords, and they built a cotton factory and a hotel at Cheekpoint, but these ventures failed, and as a result Cornelius was forced to sell his estate at Faithlegg in 1819.[4] The Boltons intermarried with the Hassard, Alcock, Newport and Barker families, and members of each of these families served on Waterford Corporation at some point in the late 18th and early 19th century.

CORNELIUS HENRY BOLTON, heir and eldest son of Cornelius Bolton of Faithlegg, Co. Waterford. He served with his father on Waterford Corporation and Waterford Chamber of Commerce.

MICHAEL EVELYN, a prominent conservative Protestant and a supporter of Alcock had, prior to the compact, been rewarded for his loyalty to the Alcock faction by being appointed to the position of corporation law agent.[5]

Right Honourable SIR JOHN NEWPORT — see first chapter.

EDMUND SKOTTOWE was a supporter of Newport. He was also a merchant and a member of Waterford Chamber of Commerce.[6]

SIR NICHOLAS BRITIFFE SKOTTOWE, a liberal Protestant, a member of the Newport faction, and a supporter of the Catholic cause.[7] In 1812, he was appointed to the position of butter taster by the corporation, a lucrative position he retained until his death in 1841, the duties of which were carried out by his deputy, Richard Curtis.[8] In the period from 1821 to 1833 Sir Nicholas received £1,615 and his deputy received £2,045.[9] Sir Nicholas established a bank with

Abraham Atkins, and from 1809 they were joined by Richard Roberts, but little is known about this venture.[10] Skottowe was a member of Waterford Chamber of Commerce and sought to reconcile differences between the chamber and the corporation.[11]

JAMES WALLACE, in addition to serving as a member of Waterford Corporation, was a revenue collector and a director of Inland Navigation for Ireland.[12] He was a conservative and a supporter of the Alcock faction on the corporation.[13]

Waterford Chamber of Commerce

EDWARD COURTENAY was a Quaker. His father, JOHN, was a partner in the merchant firm of Strangman, Courtenay and Ridgeway – all Quaker families.[14] This firm handled a large part of the export trade in the port of Waterford.[15] Joshua Strangman left the partnership in 1786. Each family continued in the overseas trade independently of each other, and most of the butter exported through Waterford was handled by these three firms.[16] In 1826, Edward Courtenay gave evidence before the parliamentary enquiry into the Irish butter trade.[17] His brother, John, operated in London, acting as an agent in the disposal of Irish butter on the London market.[18]

FRANCIS DAVIS was a merchant. When he appeared as a witness before the select committee on the butter trade he stated that he was 'extensively concerned in the corn trade'.[19]

RICHARD DAVIS was a merchant in the firm of Davis & Sons, Brewers.[20]

JOHN HARRIS was a bacon merchant.[21] When Newport's bank collapsed in 1820, Harris and the Catholic merchant, Thomas Meagher, Jnr, were appointed principal assignees.[22] Harris was an alderman on the corporation from 1832, and mayor in 1836/7;[23] he was a liberal Protestant,[24] and a support of parliamentary reform and poor relief.[25]

HENRY HOLDSWORTH HUNT, a liberal Protestant,[26] was a merchant and banker, and partner in the firm Hunt, O'Brien and Hunt. He was one of the signatories of the 1808 declaration organized by Waterford's liberal Protestants in support of the removal of restrictions on Catholics.[27] Hunt served as mayor of the city in 1826/7.[28]

ROBERT JACOB – the Chamber records state that Robert Jacob was a member of the firm of Thomas, R. & J. Jacob, timber merchants.

JOHN LEONARD was a Catholic merchant, and a member of the Catholic Association.[29]

GEORGE PENROSE RIDGWAY, of Blenheim, Co. Waterford, was the son of Henry Ridgway, of Queen's County and Elizabeth, daughter of George Penrose, Brook Lodge, Co. Waterford. The Ridgways were a Quaker family and

George's father Henry had been one of the founders of the overseas merchant company of Strangman, Courtenay and Ridgway.[30]

JEREMIAH RYAN, a prominent Catholic, was a wine merchant in Bailey's New Street, Waterford.[31] In 1799, Ryan was one of a committee of five elected at a general meeting of Roman Catholics of Waterford to prepare a declaration on the proposed legislative union between Britain and Ireland.[32]

JOHN STRANGMAN, a Quaker, was a son of Joshua Strangman (see entry for Edward Courtenay above) and was involved in the overseas trade, and the shipbuilding business.[33]

JOSEPH STRANGMAN, a Quaker, also a son of Joshua Strangman (see entry for Edward Courtenay above) and was involved in the overseas trade, and the shipbuilding business.[34]

Clonmel merchants and inhabitants

ROBERT BANFIELD, a Quaker merchant, of New Quay, Clonmel, was one of the principal merchants involved in the bacon trade. Sometime after 1802, he became a partner in the Clonmel bank operated by the Quaker family, the Watsons.[35] This bank rivalled the Riall family bank in the early 19th century, but by 1809 Watson and Co. had failed, in part because 'they ill-advisedly made loans on the security of land which fluctuated in value as the fortunes of the Napoleonic wars ebbed and flowed'.[36] Banfield also operated as an insurance agent for a number of companies, including the British and United Fire Insurance Company and the Westminster Society.[37]

ROBERT GRUBB – Three brothers of the Quaker Grubb family, JOSEPH (1710–82), a miller, JOHN (1712–79), a clothier, and BENJAMIN (1727–1802), a grocer, entered into commercial life in Clonmel in the mid-18th century, at a time when the town was entering a period of economic expansion.[38] Their descendants formed three major branches of the family in Co. Tipperary. They were intermarried with many of the families to the forefront of Quaker entrepreneurship – Joseph's son, also named Joseph, married Sarah Ridgeway of Waterford, and his daughter Rebecca married Joseph Strangman, marriage alliances most likely made to cement the common interest of these families in the export of wool.[39] The Grubb family operated the Anner Mills and six other milling businesses in and around Clonmel.[40] Robert Grubb was involved in the milling industry, and was also in the bacon business.[41] When Edward Wakefield visited Clonmel in 1809 he described a thriving bacon business and noted that the merchants involved in the trade were mainly Quakers.[42] The development of the river Suir between Clonmel and the outer harbour was central to the Grubbs' commercial interests.[43]

DAVID MALCOMSON (1765–1844), a Quaker and a native of Lurgan, came to Clonmel in 1784 to work for his cousin, Sarah Grubb, at Anner Mills,

Clonmel.[44] Malcomson made good use of a legacy he received, made many commercial and political connections, reinvested his profits and expanded his business interests. In 1790, he became the agent of Colonel John Bagwell, who operated a corn mill outside Clonmel.[45] Bagwell was one of the most significant property owners in Clonmel and became involved in politics, controlling the borough corporation.[46] Through this connection Malcomson became a freeman of the borough of Clonmel and benefited from the attendant commercial privileges.[47] In 1795, Malcomson married Mary Fennell, daughter of Joshua and Sarah Fennell, millers in Cahir, and her dowry brought him £1,500 and an estate at Crohane.[48] With the assistance of his brother John, a leading grocery and linen merchant and partner in the firm Malcomson and Riall, distillers, David Malcomson purchased the Corporation Mills on Suir Island, Clonmel for £3,000.[49] He became involved in a number of other commercial enterprises, including a grocery business and he acquired four corn mills.[50] Malcomson's property and stock portfolio was valued at £67,434 in 1816.[51] In the year before he became a Harbour Commissioner, Malcomson's firm in Clonmel exported 8,062 hundredweight of flour and by 1829 this had increased to 80,373 hundredweight.[52] In 1824, Malcomson took over a milling business at Pouldrew in east Waterford, a decision influenced by the superior fall of water at the site compared to that at Clonmel, and the proximity to Waterford city.[53] In 1825, David Malcomson established an integrated spinning and weaving factory at Portlaw, County Waterford, one of the few Irish cotton industries to repel competition from the Lancashire cotton mills over the next fifty years.[54]

JAMES MORTON, a member of the Anglican church, and the only representative from Clonmel not a member of the Society of Friends, was a member of a Clonmel merchant family. In his capacity as president of the Clonmel Commercial Association, in April 1821, he signed a petition to the chief secretary, requesting improvements to the navigation of the river Suir.[55]

ARTHUR RIALL, a Quaker, was the son of Phineas Riall of Heywood, near Clonmel and Catherine Caldwell of Dublin.[56] Phineas operated Riall's bank in Clonmel, a business he had inherited from his father William.[57] On his death Phineas Riall left his banking business to his three sons, William, Charles and Arthur.[58] The Riall banking family of Clonmel were intermarried with the Newport banking family of Waterford – Arthur Riall and Sir John Newport were first cousins.[59] In the opening years of the 19th century, the bank did brisk business as the stamp duty paid in 1803 indicates that the bank had 36,300 notes under three guineas in circulation and 5,300 notes under ten pounds.[60] The Rialls appear to have been prudent bankers and the bank survived the financial crashes of the last quarter of the 18th century. However, Riall's bank went into liquidation in August 1820, to the detriment of its creditors.[61]

Notes

ABBREVIATIONS

Decies	*Decies: The Journal of the Waterford Archaeological and Historical Society*
JCHS	*Journal of the Cork Historical Society*
JHC	*Journal(s) of the House of Commons*
NAI	National Archives of Ireland
NLI	National Library of Ireland
RWC	*Ramsey's Waterford Chronicle/Waterford Chronicle*
TCD	Trinity College Dublin
WC	Waterford Corporation
WCC	Waterford Chamber of Commerce
WCCA	Waterford City and County Archives
WHA 1816	Waterford Harbour Act 1816
WHC	Waterford Harbour Commissioners

INTRODUCTION

1 At the first meeting of the new 40-member corporation of Waterford in November 1842, 36 of the newly elected members were Catholic and 4 Protestant. A Catholic merchant, Thomas Meagher, was elected mayor. See Eugene Broderick, 'Privilege and exclusiveness: the unreformed Corporation of Waterford, 1818–1840', *Decies*, 63 (2007), 172.

2 *Report of the Ports and Harbours Tribunal, 1930*, P 238 (Saorstát Éireann), p. 851.

3 Edmund Spenser, *The Faerie Queen, Book 4, Canto xi*. http://www.sacred-texts.com/neu/eng/fq/fq50.htm [12 June 2018].

4 J.S. Carroll, 'Old Waterford Newspapers', *Decies*, 22 (1983), 55.

5 Ned McHugh, 'The port of Drogheda 1790–1850: an era of regeneration and resurgence', *Journal of the County Louth Archaeological and Historical Society*, 26:2 (2006), 151–326.

6 Joel Mokyr & Cormac Ó Gráda, 'Poor and getting poorer? Living standards in Ireland before the Famine', *Economic History Review*, 41:2 (1988), 209–35, Cormac Ó Gráda, *Ireland: a new economic history, 1780–1939* (Oxford, 1994), and

L.M. Cullen, *Anglo-Irish trade, 1660–1800* (Manchester, 1968).

7 Eugene Broderick, *Waterford's Anglicans: religion and politics, 1819–1872* (Newcastle upon Tyne, 2009).

8 Broderick, 'Privilege and exclusiveness', *Decies*, 63 (2007), 165–76.

9 E.A. Heggs, 'The nature and development of liberal Protestantism in Waterford, 1800–42' (PhD, National University of Ireland Maynooth, 2008).

10 J.M. Hearne, 'Waterford: economy, society and politics, 1780–1852', (PhD, University College Cork, 2001).

11 Peter Solar, 'The agricultural trade of the port of Waterford, 1809–1909' in William Nolan and T.P. Power (eds), *Waterford history and society: interdisciplinary essays on the history of an Irish county* (Dublin, 1992), pp 495–518.

12 P.M. Solar, 'Shipping and economic development in 19th century Ireland', *Economic History Review*, 59:4 (Nov. 2006), 717–42.

13 Eamonn McEneaney, *A history of Waterford and its mayors from the twelfth to the twentieth-century* (Waterford, 1995).

14 Bill Irish, *Shipbuilding in Waterford, 1820–1882: a historical, technical and pictorial study* (Bray, 2005).

15 Des Cowman, *Perceptions and promotions: the role of Waterford Chamber of Commerce, 1787–1987* (Waterford, 1988).

16 Anthony Brophy, 'Port of Waterford: extracts from the records of the Waterford Harbour Commissioners from their establishment in 1816 to the Report of the Ports and Harbours Tribunal, 1930', *Decies*, 60 (2004), 151–70, and Anthony Brophy, 'Statement of Sir Henry J. Forde, chairman, Waterford Harbour Commissioners to the Port and Harbours Tribunal, 1930', *Decies*, 73 (2017), 133–9.

17 Waterford Harbour Act 1816 (56 Geo. III cap. lxiv), preamble (the act is cited hereafter as WHA 1816).

1. THE MERCANTILE, POLITICAL AND
ECONOMIC ARENA: WATERFORD PORT AND
HARBOUR IN THE EARLY 19TH CENTURY

1 Mokyr and Ó Gráda, 'Poor and getting poorer?', 210.

2 Andy Bielenberg, *Ireland and the industrial revolution, the impact of the industrial revolution on Irish industry, 1801–1922* (New York, 2009), p. 6.

3 Ibid., p. 16.

4 L.M. Cullen, 'The overseas trade of Waterford as seen from a ledger of Courtenay and Ridgway', *Journal of the Royal Society of Antiquaries of Ireland*, 88:2 (1958), 165.

5 Ibid.

6 John Mannion, 'Waterford and the south of England: spatial patterns in shipping commerce, 1766–1777', *International Journal of Maritime History*, 6:2 (1994), 115.

7 John Mannion, 'Vessels, masters and seafaring: patterns of voyages in Waterford commerce, 1766–71' in Nolan and Power (eds), *Waterford history and society*, p. 375.

8 McEneaney, *Waterford and its mayors*, p. 165.

9 Cullen, 'The overseas trade of Waterford', 167. This increase reflects internal factors in Ireland and an increasing global preference for salt pork over salt beef. See: L.M. Cullen, *Anglo-Irish trade, 1660–1800* (Manchester, 1968). p. 73.

10 Hearne, 'Waterford: economy, society and politics', p. 1.

11 Julian Walton, 'Classicism and civility', *Irish Arts Review*, 21:1 (Spring, 2004), 107.

12 McEneaney, *Waterford and its mayors*, pp 167–8.

13 Charles Smith, *The ancient and present state of the county and city of Waterford* (Dublin, 1746), pp 196–7.

14 Solar, 'The agricultural trade of the port of Waterford' in Nolan and Power (eds), *Waterford history and society*, p. 495.

15 J.B. O'Brien, 'Population, society and politics in Cork from the late-eighteenth century to 1900' in Richard Lawton and Robert Lee (eds), *Population and society in western European port cities, c.1650–1939* (Liverpool, 2002), p. 329.

16 Ibid., p. 329. This was despite the fact that Cork did not export the most popular type of butter – Carlow butter, a more delicately flavoured, lightly salted butter, exported from Waterford and Dublin. See Cullen, *Anglo-Irish trade, 1660–1800*, p. 72.

17 Cullen, 'The overseas trade of Waterford', 167.

18 O'Brien, 'Population, society and politics in Cork', pp 328–31.

19 Ibid., p. 328.

20 Robin Sweetman & Cecil Nimmons, *Port of Belfast, 1785–1985: an historical review* (Belfast, 1985), p. 6.

21 Solar, 'Shipping and economic development in 19th-century Ireland', 727.

22 Matthew Potter, *The municipal revolution in Ireland: a handbook of urban government in Ireland since 1800* (Dublin, 2011), p. 70.

23 Julian Walton, *The royal charters of Waterford* (Waterford, 1992), p. 49.

24 *The great charter of the liberties of the city of Waterford with explanatory notes to which is added a list of the mayors, bailiffs, and sheriffs of the city of Waterford, from the year 1377 to the year 1806 inclusive* (Kilkenny, 1806).

25 Hearne, 'Waterford: economy, society and politics', p. vii.

26 WCC minutes, 30 Mar. 1787 (WCCA, MS W COC 1/01).

27 WCC minutes, 7 June 1805 (WCCA, MS WCOC 1/02).

28 Ibid.

29 Heggs, 'The nature and development of liberal Protestantism in Waterford', p. 58.

30 R.J. Bennett, *Local business voice: the history of chambers of commerce in Britain, Ireland and revolutionary America, 1760–2011* (Oxford, 2011), p. 3.

31 Ibid., p. 6.

32 Ibid., p. 113 & pp 156–7.

33 Virginia Crossman, *Local government in 19th-century Ireland* (Belfast, 1994), p. 4.

34 Cowman, *Perceptions and promotions*, p. 13.

35 *First report of the commissioners appointed to inquire into the municipal corporations in Ireland*, H.C. 1835 [23] [24] [25] [27] [28] xxvii, 590–1 (hereafter cited as *First report into municipal corporations in Ireland*). The report recommended reform and heralded the enactment of the Municipal Corporations (Ireland) Act, 1840, 3 & 4 Vict., c. 108 [U.K.] (10 Aug. 1840).

36 Ibid., p. 591.

37 Ibid.

38 Ibid.

39 Cowman, *Perceptions and promotions*, pp 15–18.

40 Bennett, *Local business voice*, p. 253.

41 R.J. Bennett (ed.), *Documents of the first chambers of commerce in Britain and Ireland, 1767–1839* (Oxford, 2017), p. 37. The building was erected in 1785 to a design of the Waterford born architect John Roberts. See http://www.buildingsofireland.ie/niah [16 Apr. 2018].

42 Bennett, *Local business voice*, p. 253. A list of the members of WCC in 1815 is attached at Appendix 1.

43 WCC minutes, 6 Oct. 1806 (WCCA, MS W COC 1/02).

44 Ibid., 19 Dec. 1806.

45 Ibid., 6 Oct. 1806.

46 The Directors General of Inland Navigation, established by the Irish parliament on the eve of the Act of Union in 1800, had a budget of £500,000 to expend on improving the canals and navigable waterways of Ireland and improving the port of Dublin. Their functions, and all the property vested in them, passed to the Commissioners for Public Works when that body was established by law in 1831. See: V.T.H. Delany and D.R. Delany, *The canals of the south of Ireland* (Newton Abbot, 1966), p. 21.

47 'Copies of all Reports made by the Directors General of Inland Navigation to the Lord Lieutenant of Ireland, and other Papers relative to the obstructions in the navigation of the river Suir below Waterford, from the 20 of December 1806 to the 30 May 1807' in House of Commons, *Finance accounts of Ireland for the year ended 5 January 1812*, pp 298–302, (hereafter cited as 'Reports made by the Directors General from the 20 of December 1806 to the 30 May 1807').

48 C.M. Tenison, 'The private bankers of Cork and the south of Ireland', *JCHS*, 2:15 (1893), p. 47.

49 Ibid., p. 46.

50 McEneaney, *Waterford and its mayors*, pp 167–8.

51 Broderick, *Waterford's Anglicans*, p. 137.

52 Sir John Newport, MP. Letters to officers of the Waterford Chamber of Commerce, (TCD), MS IE TCD 11342/15 and Chamber of Commerce letter books, 1800–23, WCCA, MS WCOC 20.

53 Broderick, 'Privilege and exclusiveness', 166.

54 Ibid.

55 *First report into municipal corporations in Ireland*, H.C. 1835 [23] [24] [25] [27] [28] xxvii, 1.

56 'Reports made by the Directors General from the 20 of December 1806 to the 30 May 1807', p. 298.

57 Ibid., p. 299.

58 Ibid., p. 298.

59 Ibid.

60 Cormac Ó Gráda, *Ireland: a new economic history* (Oxford, 1994), p. v.

61 Ibid., p. 5.

62 Hearne, 'Waterford: economy, society and politics', p. 2.

63 Ibid.

64 Ibid., p. 8.

65 Ibid., p. 10.

66 Ibid., p. 12.

67 *Reports by Directors General of Inland Navigation in Ireland on canals, navigable rivers and Shannon navigation, 1809–12*, H.C. 1812 (366), v, 286.

68 'Waterford port improvement petition' presented to parliament 16 Feb. 1816, see *JHC from 1 February 1816 to 2 January 1817 in the fifty-sixth year of the reign of King George the Third – sess. 1816, vol. 71*

(London, 1816), p. 51, (henceforth cited as 'Waterford port improvement petition').

69 'Waterford port improvement petition', p. 51.

70 Ibid.

71 Ibid.

72 Ibid.

73 Hearne, 'Waterford: economy, society and politics', p. x.

74 'Waterford port improvement petition', p. 51.

75 Ibid.

76 Ibid.

77 H.A. Gilligan, *A history of the port of Dublin* (Dublin, 1988), p. 51.

78 House of Commons, 2 June 1819, *JHC from 4 August 1818 to 2 November 1819, Sess. 1819, vol. 74* (London, 1819), p. 490.

79 An Act to raise a Fund for defraying the Charge of Commercial Improvements within the City and Port of Cork, in Ireland [14th July 1814.] (54 Geo. III cap. 196).

80 'Waterford port improvement petition', p. 51.

81 House of Commons 14 & 15 Mar. 1816 – *JHC from 1 February 1816 to 2 January 1817 in the fifty-sixth year of the reign of King George the Third – sess. 1816, vol. 71* (London, 1816), p. 201.

82 Ibid.

83 Heggs, 'The nature and development of liberal Protestantism in Waterford', pp 114–15.

84 House of Commons, 20 Mar. 1816 – *JHC from 1 February 1816 to 2 January 1817*, p. 230. From the act of union until 5 January 1817 Ireland and Great Britain retained separate treasuries. See: S.J. Connolly, 'Union government, 1812–1823' in W.E. Vaughan (ed.), *A new history of Ireland, v: Ireland under the union, 1801–1870* (Oxford, 1989), p. 63.

85 *First report into municipal corporations in Ireland*, 51–73 [23] [24] [25] [27] [28] H.C. 1835, xxvii.1, 51, see: Appendix 1 of report, p. 39.

2. THE ESTABLISHMENT OF WATERFORD HARBOUR COMMISSIONERS IN 1816

1 House of Commons, 20 Mar. 1816 – *JHC from 1 February 1816 to 2 January 1817*, p. 278. The ship owners and ship masters of colliers and others ships trading in and out of Waterford submitted a petition in support of the provisions of the bill. Ibid., pp 312–13.

2 WCC minute book, 1 Apr. 1816 (WCCA, WCOC 3/01).

3 *RWC*, 1 Apr. 1816.

4 Ibid., 6 Apr. 1816.

5 Ibid.

6 Ibid., 16 Apr. 1816.

7 Ibid.

8 Ibid.

9 Ibid.

10 Ibid. The practise of publishing draft bills was not in place in 1816 and therefore a copy of the draft bill is not held by the Parliamentary Archives.

11 Ibid., 20 Apr. 1816.

12 Ibid.

13 Ibid.

14 Ibid.

15 Ibid.

16 Niall Byrne (ed.), *The great parchment book of Waterford: liber antiquissimus Civitatis Waterfordiae* (Dublin, 2007), pp 41–2.

17 *Waterford Mail*, 7 Dec. 1842.

18 WHC undated and unattributed legal/correspondence documentation (NAI, WAT 28. Box 17, pp 6–9).

19 WHC Proceedings of General meetings, 31 July 1816 (NAI, WAT 28) and WC Minute Book, 30 June 1817 (WCCA, MS LA1/1/A/15). The agreement was signed by John Harris and John Strangman, two of the proposed commissioners named in the bill as representing the Chamber of Commerce, and Cornelius Bolton, Nicholas B. Skottowe and Edmund Skottowe, proposed as commissioners representing Waterford Corporation.

20 Ibid. Approximately £19,000 in present day values.

21 WHC undated and unattributed legal/correspondence documentation (NAI, WAT 28. Box 17, pp 6–9).

22 WHC Proceedings of General meetings, 31 July 1816 (NAI, WAT 28).

23 Ibid. Assumed to refer to Schedule D – Water Bailiff's fees, cited in the agreement of 15 May 1816 and omitted from the Act passed by parliament on 20 June 1816.

24 WHA 1816, section xli.

25 House of Commons, 20 Mar, 1816 – *JHC from 1 February 1816 to 2 January 1817*, p. 450.

26 WHA 1816.

27 Ibid., preamble.

28 Ibid., preamble and section vii.

29 Sweetman & Nimmons, *Port of Belfast, 1785–1985*, p. 4.

30 McHugh, 'The port of Drogheda 1790–1850', 176.

31 An Act for reviving, amending, and making perpetual, an Act passed in the Parliament of Ireland in the Fortieth Year of the Reign of His present Majesty, for the better Regulation of the Butter Trade of the City of Cork and the Liberties thereof (53 George III, c. 53). The act of 1813 in respect of the port of Cork reflects the close connection between the butter trade and the development of that port and harbour.

32 WHA 1816, preamble.

33 Ibid., preamble.

34 Ibid., section vi.

35 Ibid.

36 WHC Proceedings of General meetings, 13 Feb. 1823 (NAI, WAT 28).

37 WHC Proceedings of General meetings, 1816–42 (NAI, WAT 28) and WHC undated and unattributed legal/correspondence documentation (NAI, WAT 28. Box 17, p.3).

38 Gilligan, *A history of the port of Dublin*, p. 51.

39 Ibid.

40 WHA 1816. Section iv provided for the appointment of pilots under the direction of the Corporation of Trinity House, Deptford Strond, Kent.

41 House of Commons, 20 Mar. 1816 – *JHC from 1 February 1816 to 2 January 1817 in the fifty-sixth year of the reign of King George the Third – sess. 1816, vol. 71* (London, 1816), p. 230.

42 WHA 1816, section vi – the rate of interest on the loan was not to exceed 5 per cent per annum.

43 Ibid., section vii.

44 Ibid.

45 Ibid., section xli.

46 WC Minute Book, 30 June 1817 (WCCA, MS LA1/1/A/15).

47 Anthony Brophy, 'Statement of Sir Henry J Forde, Chairman, Waterford

Harbour Commissioners to the Ports and Harbours Tribunal, 1930', *Decies*, 73 (2017), 133–9, at 135.

48 McHugh, 'The port of Drogheda 1790–1850', 176–9.

49 Ibid., p. 179.

50 *Report of the Ports and Harbours Tribunal, 1930*, P 238 (Saorstát Éireann), p. 364.

51 Ibid., preamble and section i.

52 Ibid.

53 Ibid.

54 Appendix 3 above contains a profile of the first commissioners appointed under the WHA 1816.

55 Rosemary Sweet, *The English town, 1680–1840: government, society and culture* (Oxford, 2014), p. 43.

56 Potter, *The municipal revolution in Ireland*, pp 34–5.

57 Broderick, 'Privilege and exclusiveness', 165.

58 Potter, *The municipal revolution in Ireland*, p. 80.

59 Heggs, 'The nature and development of liberal Protestantism in Waterford', p. 48 & p. 67.

60 Broderick, 'Privilege and exclusiveness', 165–6.

61 H.F. Morris, 'The principal inhabitants of County Waterford in 1746' in Nolan & Power (eds), *Waterford history and society*, p. 316.

62 Broderick, 'Privilege and exclusiveness', 166.

63 Heggs, 'The nature and development of liberal Protestantism in Waterford', p. 168.

64 Bennett, *Documents of the first chambers of commerce*, pp 688–9.

65 Tenison, 'The private bankers of Cork', 46–7.

66 WHC undated and unattributed legal/correspondence documentation headed 'Constitution of Waterford Harbour Commissioners' (NAI, WAT 28. Box 17).

67 Sean O'Donnell, *Clonmel, 1840–1900: anatomy of an Irish town* (Dublin, 1998), p. 20.

68 Tom Hunt, 'The origin and development of the Portlaw cotton industry, 1825–1840', *Decies*, 53 (1997), 17.

69 Bielenberg, *Ireland and the Industrial Revolution*, p. 60.

70 Hunt, 'The Portlaw cotton industry', 17.

71 WHA 1816, preamble.

3. SHAPING THE PORT: IMPLEMENTING THE ACT OF 1816

1   Waterford Harbour Act, 1846 9 & 10 Vict., c. 292.
2   WHC Proceedings of General meetings, 17 July 1816 (NAI, WAT 28).
3   Ibid.
4   Ibid., 31 July 1816.
5   Ibid. The committee consisted of Edward Courtenay, John Strangman, John Leonard, Robert Jacob (commissioners representing Waterford Chamber of Commerce) and James Wallace (representing Waterford Corporation).
6   Ibid., 28 Aug. 1816. This building was to be the home of Waterford Harbour Commissioners until the year 2004.
7   Cowman, *Perceptions and promotions*, p. 19.
8   WHA 1816, schedule C.
9   WHC Proceedings of General meetings, 28 July 1816 (NAI, WAT 28).
10   Ibid., 21 Aug. 1816.
11   Ibid.
12   WHC Pilots' Journals, 1816–41, 1 Nov. 1816 (NAI, WAT 28/7).
13   WHC Minutes of Pilot Committee, 28 & 29 Oct. 1816 (NAT WAT 28/1).
14   WHC Pilots' Journals, 1816–41, 1 Nov. 1816 (NAI, WAT 28/7).
15   Ibid., 3 Nov. 1816.
16   Ibid., 8 Mar. 1822.
17   WHC Minutes of Pilot Committee, 28 & 29 Oct. 1816 (NAT WAT 28/1).
18   *Tidal Harbours Commissioners: second report of the commissioners, with minutes of evidence, appendices, supplement and index*, p. 90, H.C. 1846 [692], xviii (hereinafter cited as *Tidal Harbours Commissioners*).
19   *RWC*, 1 Apr. 1816.
20   WHA 1816, schedule A.
21   WHC Proceedings of General meetings, 7 Aug. 1816 (NAI WAT 28).
22   Ibid.
23   Ibid., 28 Oct. 1816.
24   *Waterford Mail*, 7 Dec. 1842.
25   Ibid.
26   Ibid.
27   Ibid. (Irish currency).
28   Ibid. Evelyn gave this information in evidence to the commissioners inquiring into municipal corporations.
29   WHC Proceedings of General meetings, 9 Oct. 1816 (NAI, WAT 28).
30   Tenison, 'The private bankers of Cork', 46–8. In 1808 the value of the bank's notes in the hands of the public was £150,000.
31   Ibid.
32   R.H. Ryland, *The history, topography and antiquities of the county and city of Waterford* (London, 1824), p. 105.
33   *Tenth report of the commissioners for auditing public accounts in Ireland*, p. 24, H.C. 1822 (51), vii, 579.
34   *Eleventh report of the commissioners for auditing public accounts in Ireland*, p. 24, H.C. 1823 (199), x, 129.
35   *Twelfth report of the commissioners for auditing public accounts in Ireland*, p. 23, H.C. 1824 (155), xxii, 287; *Fourteenth report of the commissioners for auditing public accounts in Ireland*, p. 22, H.C. 1826 (317), xi, 309, and *Twentieth report of the commissioners for auditing public accounts in Ireland*, p. 20, H.C. 1832 (75), xxiii, 1.
36   Ibid., p. 21. In the accounts for year ended 5/1/1832 the sum owing to the commissioners is stated at £1,826 1s. 1d. Two further small payments were made by the assignees of Newport's Bank in the year ended 31/3/1840 – see Accounts for year ended 31/3/1840 WHC Accounts (NAI, WAT 28 Box 3).
37   WHA 1816, – rates set out in schedules attached to the act.
38   Ibid.
39   *RWC*, 1 Apr. 1816.
40   WHC Proceedings of General meetings, 11 Sept. 1818 (NAI, WAT 28).
41   Ibid., 11 Mar. 1824 (NAI, WAT 28). Rates on coasters not exceeding 50 tons had been reduced from 5 April 1821.
42   An Act for erecting a Ballast Office, and for regulating Pilots within the Port and Harbour of Cork; and for rendering more safe and commodious the said Port and Harbour for all Ships and Vessels trading to and from the same, 1820 (1 Geo. IV., c. 52).
43   WHC Statement showing the receipts and expenditure of the commissioners under the Act of 1816 for improving the port and harbour of Waterford taken from the accounts as certified by the commissioners for auditing public accounts – Statement of gross income and expenditure 1 September 1816

to 31 March 1837 (NAI, WAT 28/7 Expenditure and other journals 1816–42).

44 Ibid. The Irish currency was assimilated to that of the British with effect from 5 Jan. 1826 and accordingly the income and expenditure data for 1816 to 1826 has been converted to British currency by the commissioners at the rate of .9230 or 13:12 Irish to British.

45 McHugh, 'The port of Drogheda 1790–1850', 185.

46 *Tidal Harbours Commissioners*, p. 94.

47 Ibid.

48 *Seventh report of the commissioners for auditing public accounts in Ireland*, p. 25, H.C. 1819 (422), xii, 501.

49 *Tenth report of the commissioners for auditing public accounts in Ireland*, p. 24, H.C. 1822 (51), vii, 579.

50 *Twelfth report of the commissioners for auditing public accounts in Ireland*, p. 23, H.C. 1824 (155), xxii, 287.

51 *Thirteenth report of the commissioners for auditing public accounts in Ireland*, p. 21, H.C. 1826 (185), xi, 177.

52 *Eighteenth report of the commissioners for auditing public accounts in Ireland*, p. 11, H.C. 1830 (323), xv, 419.

53 *Nineteenth report of the commissioners for auditing public accounts in Ireland*, p. 23, H.C. 1831 (12), x, 185.

54 *Twentieth report of the commissioners for auditing public accounts in Ireland*, p. 20, H.C. 1832 (75), xxiii, 1.

55 *Twenty-first report of the commissioners for auditing public accounts in Ireland*, p. 21, H.C. 1833 (102), xvii, 1.

56 *Municipal Corporations (Ireland). Appendix to the First Report of the Commissioners* Part I, H.C. 1835 [27, 28], xxvii.

57 *Waterford Mail*, 4 June 1834.

58 *Waterford Chronicle*, 15 July 1837.

59 *Waterford Mail*, 6 Feb. 1839.

60 WHC Proceedings of General meetings, 23 Feb. 1821, 8 Nov. 1821 and 13 Feb. 1823. (NAI, WAT 28).

61 *Eleventh report of the commissioners for auditing public accounts in Ireland*, p. 24, H.C. 1823 (199), x, 129.

62 Ibid.

63 Ibid.

64 Ibid.

65 *Thirteenth report of the commissioners for auditing public accounts in Ireland*, p. 21, H.C. 1825 (185), XI, 177.

66 *Eighteenth report of the commissioners for auditing public accounts in Ireland*, p. 21, H.C. 1830 (323), xv, 419.

67 WHA 1816, preamble and section vi – the rate of interest on the loan was not to exceed 5 per cent per annum.

68 WHA 1816, section vii.

69 Ibid.

70 WHC Proceedings of General meetings, 17 July 1816 (NAI, WAT 28).

71 'Waterford port improvement petition', p. 51.

72 Letter from the Board of Inland Navigation to George Brownrigg, Secretary of WHC dated 9 Dec. 1816. WHC loose, uncatalogued correspondence and documentation (NAI, WAT 28. Box 17).

73 WHC Pilots' Journals, 1816–41 (NAI, WAT 28/7).

74 *Tidal Harbours Commissioners*, Appendix A, p. 48a.

75 Ibid.

76 *Returns of all sums of money voted or applied, either by way of grant or loan, in aid of public works in Ireland, since the union*, p. 69. H.C. 1839 (540), xliv, 493.

77 *JHC, 1830*, vol. 85, p. 38.

78 WHC Proceedings of General meetings, 19 Nov. 1829. (NAI, WAT 28). The minutes recorded that the pilot committee and the Law Agent had drawn up a draft bill – this draft could not be located. It was resolved on 14 January 1830 to submit a petition to parliament supporting amendments to 'the Harbour Act'.

79 WHC Proceedings of General meetings, 17 Sept., 1829.

80 *JHC, 1830*, vol. 85, p. 38. The commissioners employed six watchmen who were stationed on the quays at night for 'the saving of person from drowning, the general protection of shipping & the property of this board from nightly pilfering' – see WHC Proceedings of General meetings, 14 Feb. 1822. (NAI, WAT 28). In 1829 the commissioners agreed to appoint an additional watchman to work during the day to prevent nuisances on the quays and protect stages and planks. Ibid., 19 Nov. 1829.

81 *JHC, 1830*, vol. 85, p. 53.

82 *Waterford Mail*, 3 Apr. 1830 – contains a copy of the draft bill presented to parliament.

83 Ibid.

84 Ibid.

85 *RWC*, 1 Apr. 1830. It would emerge that the proposal was to reduce from 13 to 10 the number of members required to make bye-laws – see *Waterford Mail*, 8 May 1830. Note: Fogarty was the principal agent of the Catholic merchant Thomas Meagher – prior to Meagher's return to Waterford in 1817. See F.G. Halpenny, *Dictionary of Canadian biography, vol. 8, 1836–1850* (Toronto, 1988), p. 597. Meagher, a wealthy Catholic merchant and father of Thomas Francis Meagher, became the first post-Reformation Catholic mayor of Waterford in 1842, following reform of the municipal corporation system.

86 *Waterford Mail*, 9 July 1828.

87 *Waterford Mail*, 26 July 1828.

88 *RWC*, 1 Apr. 1830.

89 Ibid.

90 McHugh, 'The port of Drogheda 1790–1850', 307.

91 Broderick, *Waterford's Anglicans*, p. 171 – Broderick asserts that in the years after 1830 relationships between Catholics and liberal Protestant deteriorated.

92 WHC Proceedings of General meetings, 1 Apr. 1830 (NAI, WAT 28).

93 Ibid.

94 Ibid., 29 Apr. 1830.

95 *Waterford Mail*, 8 May 1830.

96 Ibid.

97 Ibid.

98 Ibid.

99 Ibid., 15 May 1830.

100 *Tidal Harbours Commissioners*, p. 93.

101 WHC Proceedings of General meetings, 21 May 1838 (NAI, WAT 28).

102 *Tidal Harbours Commissioners*, Mr William Cubitt's report to Waterford Harbour Commissioners dated 31 July 1838, pp 93–5.

103 *Tidal Harbours Commissioners*, p. 93. Cork purchased a steam dredging vessel in 1826 and by 1832, 182,877 tons of material had been lifted. They purchased a second dredger in 1839 – see Mary Leland, *Port of Cork,*

that endless adventure: a history of the Cork Harbour Commissioners (Cork, 2001), p. 56. Drogheda introduced mechanized dredging in 1827 at a cost of £5,000 – see McHugh, 'The port of Drogheda 1790–1850', 182.

104 *Tidal Harbours Commissioners*, p. vi.

105 WHA 1816, preamble.

106 WHC Pilots' Journals, 1816–41 (NAI, WAT 28/7).

107 *Third report of the commissioners of inquiry into the collection and management of the revenue arising in Ireland*, pp 34–5, H.C. 1822 (606) xiii.

108 *Accounts, showing the amount of customs duties collected, the number and tonnage of vessels entering and clearing outwards, and the number and tonnage of vessels registered, in each of the several ports of Ireland, for each of the ten years ending January 1850*, p. 499, H.C. 1851 (171) l, 493 (hereafter referred to as *Accounts showing the number and tonnage of vessels registered, in each of the several ports of Ireland, for each of the ten years ending January 1850*).

109 *Third report of the commissioners of inquiry into the collection and management of the revenue arising in Ireland*, pp 34–5, H.C. 1822 (606) xiii.

110 *Accounts showing the number and tonnage of vessels registered, in each of the several ports of Ireland, for each of the ten years ending January 1850*, p. 499, H.C. 1851 (171) l, 493.

111 Irish, *Shipbuilding in Waterford, 1820–1882*, p. 29.

112 Ibid.

113 Ibid., p. 31.

114 Ibid., p. 145.

115 Ibid., p. 141.

116 *Tonnage of vessels (Ireland), An account of the number of vessels with their tonnage entered inwards and cleared outwards in the last five years, ending 5th January 1835*, pp 2–5, H.C. 1835 (107) xlviii, 541.

117 Ibid.

118 *Return of number of sailing and steam vessels registered at each port of Great Britain and Ireland, 1842*, p. 3, H.C. 1843 (207) lii, 393.

119 Ibid.

120 Bill Irish, 'Mail packet steamers at Waterford', *Decies*, 60 (2004), 117–50, at p. 119.

121 WHC *Proceedings of General meetings*, 18 Apr. 1826 (NAI, WAT 28).

122 Irish, *Shipbuilding in Waterford*, p. 24.

123 *First report into the municipal corporations in Ireland*, p. 605 [23] [24] [25] [27] [28] H.C. 1835, xxvii.1, 51.

124 WHC *Proceedings of General meetings*, 13 Feb. 1823 (NAI, WAT 28).

125 Ibid.

126 *Tidal Harbours Commission*, p. 95.

127 McHugh, 'The port of Drogheda 1790–1850: an era of regeneration and resurgence', 185.

128 Leland, *Port of Cork, that endless adventure*, p. 56.

CONCLUSION

1 *Accounts showing the number and tonnage of vessels registered, in each of the several ports of Ireland, for each of the ten years ending January 1850*, p. 499, H.C. 1851 (171) l, 493.

APPENDIX 1

1 Bennett, *Documents of the first chambers of commerce*, pp 688–90.

APPENDIX 3

1 http://www.historyofparliamentonline.org/volume/1820–1832/constituencies/waterford [13 May 2018].

2 McEneaney, *Waterford and its manors*, p. 233.

3 J.B. Burke, *The heraldic register, 1849–1850, with an annotated obituary* (London, 1850), p. 90.

4 Heggs, 'The nature and development of liberal Protestantism in Waterford', p. 79.

5 Ibid., p. 73.

6 Bennett, *Documents of the first chambers of commerce*, pp 688–9.

7 *Freeman's Journal*, 23 Feb. 1825.

8 *First report into municipal corporations in Ireland*, 51–73 [23] [24] [25] [27] [28] H.C. 1835, xxvii.1, 51, see: Appendix 1, p. 591.

9 Ibid.

10 C. Tenison, 'The private bankers of Cork', 47.

11 Heggs, 'The nature and development of liberal Protestantism in Waterford', p. 168.

12 *Pigott's and Co., Provincial Directory of Ireland, 1824.*

13 Heggs, 'The nature and development of liberal Protestantism in Waterford', p. 213.

14 Cullen, 'The overseas trade of Waterford', 165–6.

15 Michael Ahern, 'The Quakers of County Tipperary, 1655–1924' (PhD, National University of Ireland Maynooth, 2003), p. 274.

16 Cullen, 'The overseas trade of Waterford', 167.

17 Ibid., 167–8,

18 Ibid., 167.

19 *Report from select committee appointed to report on the butter trade of Ireland, minutes of evidence, 1826*, p. 150, H.C. 1826 (406), v, 135.

20 Bennett, *Documents of the first chambers of commerce*, pp 688–9.

21 J.M. Hearne & R.T. Cornish, *Thomas Francis Meagher: the making of an Irish American* (Dublin, 2006), p. 25.

22 Ibid.

23 McEneaney, *Waterford and its mayors*, p. 233.

24 Heggs, 'The nature and development of liberal Protestantism in Waterford', p. 297.

25 Ibid., p. 279.

26 Ibid., p. 48.

27 *Waterford Mirror*, 28 Mar. 1808.

28 McEneaney, *Waterford and its mayors*, p. 233.

29 *Waterford Mail*, 13 Nov. 1824.

30 Cullen, 'The overseas trade of Waterford', 167.

31 Brian MacDermot, *The Catholic question in Ireland and England, 1798–1822: the papers of Denys Scully* (Dublin, 1988), p. 131.

32 *Belfast Newsletter*, 17 Sept. 1799.

33 Cullen, 'The overseas trade of Waterford', p. 166.

34 Ibid., p. 168.

35 Tenison, 'The private bankers of Cork', 70.

36 S.J. Watson, *A dinner of herbs: a history of Old St Mary's Church, Clonmel* (Clonmel, 1988), p. 112.

37 Ahern, 'The Quakers of County Tipperary', p. 249.

38 Michael Ahern, 'The Grubbs – a Tipperary Quaker family', *Decies*, 56 (2000), 55–66, at 57.

39 Ahern, 'The Quakers of County Tipperary', p. 107.
40 Ibid., p. 59.
41 Ibid., p. 232.
42 Edward Wakefield, *An account of Ireland, statistical and political*, 2 vols (London, 1812), i, p. 752.
43 Ahern, 'The Grubbs – a Tipperary Quaker family', p. 60.
44 Hunt, 'The Portlaw cotton industry', 17.
45 Ahern, 'The Quakers of County Tipperary', p. 269.
46 Hunt, 'The Portlaw cotton industry', 18.
47 Ibid., 269.
48 Andy Bielenberg (ed.), *Irish flour milling: a history, 600–2000* (Dublin, 2003), p. 90.
49 Ibid.
50 Ibid.
51 Hunt, 'The Portlaw cotton industry', 18.
52 Ibid. Hunt extracted this data from 'Malcomson, family of: Notes on members of Malcomson family, originally of Armagh, in 18th and 19th centuries; with notes on family enterprises, including Lax Weir and Fishery, Limerick; Neptune Ironworks, Waterford; Portlaw Cotton Factory'. Microfilm, N.6199, P.6935.
53 Ibid., p. 19.
54 Cormac Ó Gráda, *Ireland; a new economic history, 1780–1939* (Oxford, 1994), p. 279.
55 Petition of commercial association of Clonmel, County Tipperary, requesting improvements to navigation of river Suir, April 1821, (NAI, MS CSORP 1821/76).
56 Tenison, 'The private bankers of Cork', 69. Tenison stated the surname as Callwell but from the records of the Caldwell family held in the Royal Irish Academy it appears that Catherine Caldwell married into the Riall family of Clonmel – RIA, MS 12 R 39 – RIA, MS 12 R 48.
57 Ibid. William Riall had married Mary Bagwell of the Bagwell banking and political family. Mary's brother William Bagwell was member of parliament for Clonmel.
58 Ibid.
59 W.P. Burke, *History of Clonmel* (Cahir, 1907), p. 386. Arthur Riall's aunt Elizabeth married Simon Newport, founder of Newport's bank, and father of Sir John Newport.
60 Ibid.
61 Tenison, 'The private bankers of Cork', 69.